Culturally
Considerate
SCHOOL COUNSELING

In loving memory of my mother,
Carlita Kaye Friend Anderson

Culturally
Considerate
SCHOOL COUNSELING
·············· *Helping Without Bias*

KIM L. ANDERSON
Foreword by Bonnie M. Davis

CORWIN
A SAGE Company

For information:

Corwin
A SAGE Company
2455 Teller Road
Thousand Oaks, California 91320
(800) 233-9936
Fax: (800) 417-2466
www.corwin.com

SAGE India Pvt. Ltd.
B 1/I 1 Mohan Cooperative
  Industrial Area
Mathura Road, New Delhi 110 044
India

SAGE Ltd.
1 Oliver's Yard
55 City Road
London EC1Y 1SP
United Kingdom

SAGE Asia-Pacific Pte. Ltd
33 Pekin Street #02-01
Far East Square
Singapore 048763

Printed in the United States of America

Library of Congress Cataloging-in-Publication Data

Anderson, Kim L.
Culturally considerate school counseling: helping without bias / Kim L. Anderson; foreword by Bonnie M. Davis.
    p. cm.
Includes bibliographical references and index.
ISBN 978-1-4129-8751-6 (pbk.)
   1. Educational counseling—Social aspects—United States. 2. Minority students—Counseling of—United States. 3. Multiculturalism—United States. I. Title.

LB1027.5.A6235 2011
371.4089—dc22   2010017720

This book is printed on acid-free paper.

10   11   12   13   14   10 9 8 7 6 5 4 3 2 1

Acquisitions Editor:	Jessica Allan
Associate Editor:	Joanna Coelho
Editorial Assistant:	Allison Scott
Production Editor:	Melanie Birdsall
Copy Editor:	Jeannette K. McCoy
Typesetter:	Hurix Systems
Proofreader:	Gail Fay
Cover Designer:	Scott Van Atta

Contents

Foreword

K im Anderson listens. She has spent her entire adult life listening to others: children in need of counseling, victims of abuse, and individuals alienated from family, friends, and self. She is a counselor in the truest sense of the word.

I met Kim in a creative writing class in 1999, just weeks before my mother passed away, and Kim listened to me. Immediately, we connected as women, as educators, and as soul sisters. We joked that Kim became the *midwife* for my first book, a self-published tome that morphed into *How to Teach Students Who Don't Look Like You: Culturally Relevant Teaching Strategies,* published by Corwin in 2006. We continued our relationship through the writing workshops we gave under the apt title of *Writing the Women's Way.* In these workshops, we sought to offer women a platform for writing about their life experiences where they felt validated and visible.

Kim has now written a book that validates her knowledge and makes visible all she has to offer us. Because of her life experiences, both personally and professionally, Kim has been able to create a book that reflects her years of listening combined with close scholarship, extensive research, and her keen intellect. Kim has written a rich resource for individual counselors, teachers, social workers, administrators, and every educator who works with children.

This book is a comprehensive compendium of facts and personal narratives that offers the reader the necessary resources needed to better respond to students today. With today's educators being asked to respond to a myriad of challenges, educators need facts, information, and strategies to meet the needs of the students who walk through their doors. This book offers all of these.

This book is a deeply passionate call to arms, combined with a wealth of information for educators in hope there will be "helping without bias." Implementing the eight-stage Model of Diversity Development, Kim takes us beyond where other books lead us. She offers us the necessity of reparation. As she says, "It isn't enough to verbalize awareness or even to behave without bias." Kim asks for more. We must accept a mantle of humility and offer reparation. We must "honor our humanness" and never stop learning. We must truly be lifelong learners, and this text enables us to expand our repertoire and support the health and welfare of each child who enters our door.

Kim helps us understand the art of *empathic understanding of student individuality*. She sees our differences as a "meeting point" for considering individuality in our students rather than as challenges to be overcome. In the book, she offers us practical strategies to address these differences as well as tools to understand how difference magnifies the possibilities within our student population rather than diminishing the outcomes. *Culturally Considerate School Counseling: Helping Without Bias* expands rather than limits our perceptions and our responses to our students.

Kim forces us to look beyond appellations such as *race, ethnicity*, and *culture* and consider instead the student's heritage, history, geography, circumstance, and affinity—markers that give us far more information that categorizing a student based on *race*. Kim pleads with us to connect with and get to know the student as an individual, not as a category.

Kim combines the standards of the American School Counselor Association (ASCA) National Model with the practicality of suggested strategies for implementation. Readers will come away from this book with an improved understanding of culturally considerate counseling and learn how "helping without bias" offers educators a new paradigm of meeting student needs. It is a book to transform counseling, offering a model for the 21st century.

—*Bonnie M. Davis, PhD*

Preface

It was the best of times, it was the worst of times; it was the age of wisdom, it was the age of foolishness; it was the epoch of belief, it was the epoch of incredulity; it was the season of Light, it was the season of Darkness; it was the spring of hope, it was the winter of despair; we had everything before us, we had nothing before us; we were all going directly to Heaven, we were all going the other way.

—Charles Dickens, *A Tale of Two Cities* (1859/1993, p. 1)

C hange has come to America," Barack Obama said in his presidential victory speech November 4, 2008. Those words asserted hope and dignity and invited the country to join in a contemporary state of compassion and tolerance. Like many Americans, I joined in the hope that this was a turning point. Having spent most of my life wishing for a fair and balanced nation, this moment in history seemed to signal change had indeed come.

Eight months later, the hope has not died, but brutal reality has returned. Within the month I begin to write an optimistic book about expanding cultural consideration in our school counseling programs, violence breaks out across the country, seemingly random yet deliberate in the message of hate spewed among the bullets that take the lives of dedicated individuals doing jobs in sacred places.

Topics of cultural diversity, ordinarily second nature to me, became leaden with the sadness and pointlessness of these acts of domestic terrorism. At the root of each, there was a commonality: *bias* and a disturbing lack of *consideration* of others.

So, I took a deep breath and a step back and tried to remember what it was like 30 years ago when I began this work. I took another breath and a few more steps backward and remembered what it was like when I was in my teens and another nonwar war was raging on the television each night. One more breath and several more steps and I remembered my first day of school, holding hands with a little black boy as we skipped around a May pole on a California playground. He asked quite politely, "How come you have those scars on your face?" and I replied honestly, "I don't know." I asked him, "How come your hands are a different color on the inside?" and he shrugged and said, "I don't know." Those innocent, *considerate* questions bonded us. We may not have known the answers, but our nervous curiosity had been dissipated by stating the obvious, asking questions, and accepting that some things just are what they are.

Lately, we seem to have lost our capacity to be considerate, to be "thoughtful of the rights and feelings of others" (*Merriam-Webster's*, 1973). The word "empathy" has even caused dispute—as if it is a bad thing to be empathic in our assessment of judicial right and wrongs. While our counseling office is not a courtroom and we are not judges, we do make decisions each day based upon the evidence put before us by our students. If we lack a piece of evidence or the ability to ask the right questions, we cannot adequately do our jobs or make a judgment about what course of action to take or intervention to enact. Empathy is the basic tenet of all helping professions. Without it, we are robotic and rigid; with it, we are human and humane.

Culturally Considerate School Counseling: Helping Without Bias is written to impart a simple message of acceptance, consideration, and the importance of empathic understanding of student individuality. The obvious will often be stated, questions will be asked of the reader, and ways in which to be a more culturally considerate counselor will be shared through research, case vignettes, tested strategies, and a new paradigm for professional diversity development. Helping without bias also requires self-reflection, the willingness to grow personally and professionally, and a desire to consider our differences as a meeting point for considering individuality in our student clients.

Change has come to America, and change can come to the classroom, the counseling office, and the school community. As in *A Tale of Two Cities,* change brings the best of times and the worst of times. I choose to believe we have everything before us.

Acknowledgments

Bonnie Davis befriended and believed in me since the first day we bonded over the mysteries of writing rights and righting wrongs. In the absence of her warmth and wisdom, this book would not have been published. Thank you, Bonnie.

I am grateful to Dan Alpert of Corwin who politely read my first outline and introduced me to Jessica Allan who became my editor and literary guardian angel. Thank you, Jessica. I'm a believer.

I am likewise grateful to Melanie Birdsall and Jeannette McCoy for their tireless effort to make this book come to life and to Scott Van Atta who patiently wove the cover into a colorful representation of the content. Thank you, Melanie and Scott. *Now* we can breathe, Jeannette!

There have been many teachers in my life who deserve recognition: Miss Froese in grade school, Max Tyndall in college, and Dr. Joanne Mermelstein in graduate school. Some have been with me longer than others. Mary St. Clair not only taught me about expressive arts psychotherapy but allowed me to teach at a time when I questioned not only my skills but my instincts. Thank you, Mary.

Ina Hughes gave me a refresher course in creative nonfiction and left me dancing with the muse across mesas in Abique, New Mexico. Thank you, Ina.

My best teachers have always been my clients. Grown or growing, they each taught me invaluable lessons in helping without bias. Thanks to each for the opportunity to travel with you for a while.

I must thank my brother, Mark Anderson, and my sister, Michelle Anderson Payton, for being there despite the years apart and miles between. My aunt, Karen Friend Maggard, is an underdiscovered writer and artist. When I was small, I wanted to be just like her. Thank you, Karrie, for planting those seeds of inspiration.

I have been blessed with a wonderful extended and alternate family. My beautiful soul sisters, Kathy MacIntosh and Kathy Graves, have made themselves available to me in ways I can never repay. Thank you, Katie. Thank you, Dr. Kathy. I didn't see Russia from your house, but I did see a rainbow over the Russian Orthodox Church in Ninilchik.

Lucky happenstance brought Rick Sealey into my life during college, and he returned to be a tremendous source of support and strength during my darkest days. Thank you, Rick.

Thanks to Dr. Donn Kleinschmidt and Mr. Buff Buffkin for being fabulous and faithful friends.

I am thankful for the many good days with Mr. Bernard Kuhn, who reminds me of the importance of simple pleasures and living in the present. Thank you, Dad Kuhn. Debbie Kuhn feeds my heart and soul with her kindness, character, and decadent desserts. Thank you, Miss Deb.

PUBLISHER'S ACKNOWLEDGMENTS

Corwin would like to gratefully acknowledge the contributions of the following reviewers:

Jason Breaker
Assistant Principal
Mount Tabor Middle School
Portland, OR

Rebecca M. Dedmond
Director, School Counseling
George Washington University
Alexandria, VA

Patricia Hart DeNoble, LICSW, BCD
Clinical Social Worker
Oakdale Elementary School
Dedham Public Schools
Dedham, MA

Joseph Gordon
Professional School Counselor
DuPont Hadley Middle School
Old Hickory, TN

Mary Monroe Kolek, PhD
Deputy Superintendent
New Canaan Public Schools
New Canaan, CT

Dr. Joyce Stout
School Counselor
Redondo Beach Unified School District
Redondo Beach, CA

About the Author

 **Kim L. Anderson** holds a bachelor's degree in mass media, completing both writing and photography tracks, and a minor in graphic arts. She developed an independent curriculum in media arts for social services and received a master's in social work from Washington University in St. Louis, Missouri. After a 20-year clinical career, she also obtained a postgraduate certificate in Expressive Arts Psychotherapy from the St. Louis Institute of Art Psychotherapy. Utilizing her training and experience as an expressive therapist, she returned to work with children, interfacing often with schools and educators on behalf of students, families, and communities.

While practicing as a psychotherapist, Kim co-owned a group therapy practice and was responsible for the marketing management as well as clinical coordination. She developed a certificate program in women's psychotherapy, supervising both students and professionals, and has conducted numerous training workshops and presentations for agencies, community organizations, and conferences. Kim also maintained a consulting practice, providing clinical expertise and program development to social service agencies and independent professionals. These skills, combined with writing, research, and editing experience branched into consultation with other small, socially conscious businesses and entrepreneurs.

Among her clinical specializations, Kim gained recognition for expertise in multiculturalism and diversity. For several years, she was a contributing editor for the *Social Work Journal,* the professional publication of the National Association of Social Workers, most often editing submissions addressing issues important to women and culturally diverse populations.

Kim is a published writer and poet, a photographer, and a mixed-media artist. She has presented a number of writing and creativity workshops and is a contributor to Dr. Bonnie Davis' latest book *The Biracial and Multiracial Student Experience: A Journey to Racial Literacy.* For more information, please visit Kim's website at www.helpingwithoutbias.com.

PART I

Populations to Consider

1

Culturally Considerate Counseling

I come from a long line of natural helpers guided by one simple, yet rarely spoken principle: *treat people with respect*. That basic principle also guides this book and decides its title. Perhaps to some *Culturally Considerate School Counseling: Helping Without Bias* seems passive and does not demand proficiency, yet cultural competency cannot take place without compassion and self-awareness. Grammatically, *helping* may be a gerund but in action, *helping without bias* is life affirming and happens only when helpers arrive with open rather than loaded arms.

My life was affirmed as an infant by my tenacious family of natural helpers and the blessed narcissism of a gifted young surgeon who saw to it I survived a rare congenital condition. My individual history contributes to my professional identity and converges in this volume.

Through literature, practical examples, heavily camouflaged case vignettes, and personal narrative, *Culturally Considerate School Counseling: Helping Without Bias* merges research with search for meaning. There are many models and measurements of cultural competency, yet there are few resources which address character education for professionals. At its core, cultural consideration is the golden rule existing throughout all societies. Buddhism: *Hurt not others in ways that you yourself would find hurtful.* Judaism: *Love thy neighbor as thyself.* Hinduism: *Do not do to others what would cause pain if done to you.* Christianity: *Do unto others as you would have them do unto you.* Islam: *Seek for mankind that of which you are desirous for yourself.* Lakota Sioux: *Mitakuye oyas'in* (all my relations).

3

THE ASCA NATIONAL MODEL

In 1988, the American School Counselor Association (ASCA) adopted the first position statement encouraging its membership to take a proactive stance on multiculturalism and challenged school counselors to be more critically reflective about issues of equity and diversity. In 2004, a new statement was adopted, directing professional school counselors to "advocate for appropriate opportunities and services that promote maximum development for all students regardless of cultural backgrounds and strive to remove barriers impeding student success" (Ravitch, 2006). Professional school counselors are urged to accomplish this by

- increasing awareness of culturally diverse persons and populations,
- increasing sensitivity of students and parents to cultural diversity, and
- enhancing the total school and community climate for all students. (American School Counselor Association, 1988, 1993, 1999, 2004)

The ASCA relies upon *The ASCA National Model: A Framework for School Counseling* for guidance and mandates regarding the professional school counseling profession. The ASCA National Model "maximizes the full potential of the National Standards document and addresses education reform efforts." The model also "incorporates school counseling standards for every student, to meet the needs of all students, and to close the gap between specific groups of students and their peers" (American School Counselor Association, 2005).

The preamble of the Ethical Standards for School Counselors states that "professional school counselors are advocates, leaders, collaborators, and consultants who create opportunities for equity in access and success in educational opportunities" (American School Counselor Association, 2005). The categories of responsibilities outlined by these ethical standards are as follows:

a. Responsibilities to Students

b. Responsibilities to Parents and/or Guardians

c. Responsibilities to Colleagues and Professional Associates

d. Responsibilities to the School and Community

e. Responsibility to Self

f. Responsibility to the Profession

g. Maintenance of Standards

Each of these responsibilities inherently includes competencies in multiculturalism and diversity, yet only one, Responsibility to Self (E.2.)

specifies *diversity* and provides the following standards for professional school counselors:

a. Affirms the diversity of students, staff, and families

b. Expands and develops awareness of his or her own attitudes and beliefs affecting cultural values and biases and strives to attain cultural competencies

c. Possesses knowledge and understanding about how oppression, racism, discrimination, and stereotyping affect him or her personally and professionally

d. Acquires educational, consultation and training, experiences to improve awareness, knowledge, skills and effectiveness in working with diverse populations: ethnic and/or racial status, age, economic status, special needs, ESL or ELL, immigration status, sexual orientation, gender, gender identity and/or expression, family type, religious and/or spiritual identity, and appearance (American School Counselor Association, 2005)

Culturally Considerate School Counseling: Helping Without Bias incorporates wisdom from a variety of sources, representing a number of disciplines and theories, none more important than that of the ASCA. Whenever possible, cultural competencies will be drawn from the tenets of the ASCA National Model, and strategies will be suggested to facilitate and achieve them. The ASCA framework is similar to the ethical standards of school psychologists, school social workers, and other allied professions. Cultural competencies and supportive strategies should easily transfer to these professions as well.

In *Multiculturalism and Diversity: School Counseling Principles*, Ravitch (2006) asserts that organizing data on the basis of specific racial, cultural, or ethnic groups compartmentalizes students by one aspect of their identity rather than looking at students, counselors, schools, and communities more holistically. Similarly, I prefer a more expansive language for exploring issues of difference and taking notice of populations to consider. Some terms cannot be avoided without resorting to laborious and awkward exposition, but we can learn to use them in less limiting ways. Research shows this is quickly becoming essential.

RACE, ETHNICITY, AND CULTURE

There is a great debate about the words "race," "ethnicity," and "culture," and there are many knowledgeable and eloquent scholars who address the complex history and science surrounding them, yet these terms remain in our daily vernacular. Anthropologists have led the way in redefining how we think and speak about racial categories, and social scientists have added opinions from sociological and psychological perspectives. In short, these words—categories—are becoming obsolete.

In 1996, the *American Journal of Physical Anthropology* published the following statement on the biological aspects of race:

> These old racial categories were based on externally visible traits, primarily skin color, features of the face, and the shape and size of the head and body, and the underlying skeleton. They were often imbued with nonbiological attributes, based on social constructs of race . . . such notions have often been used to support racist doctrines. (American Association of Physical Anthropologists, 1996)

"Ethnicity" may be more appropriate by definition but equally inadequate if not insensitive.

> Ethnicity refers to clusters of people who have common . . . traits . . . and view themselves as constituting an ethnic group, . . . but ethnic groups and ethnicity are not fixed, bounded entities; they are open, flexible, and subject to change, and they are usually self-defined. (Smedley & Smedley, 2005)

The United States Census Bureau provides more authoritative data on the subject of the "American Community," interchanging ancestry with "ethnic origin or descent" and "heritage or country of birth of person or ancestors." The census data of 2000 yielded seven basic categories: White, Black or African American, American Indian and Alaskan Native, Asian, Native Hawaiian and Other Pacific Islander, Some Other Race, and Two or More Races (U.S. Census Bureau, 2009). Tidy perhaps, but neither exhaustive nor inclusive.

The federal government considers race and Hispanic origin to be two separate and distinct concepts, asserting that Hispanics and Latinos may be of "any race." In fact, there is disagreement within Hispanic/Latino communities and between generations and gender about which term is preferred (Hede, 2009). Dotson-Blake, Foster, and Gressard (2009) state the term "Hispanic" is regarded by many as being inadequate for use as a total population descriptor as it neglects to address unique identities of individuals from Mexico, Central and South America, and Spanish-speaking Caribbean. Immigrants from these areas often identify more strongly with their nationality than with their language. The terms "Latino"/"Latina" have become more widely accepted in an effort to establish an identity with Latin cultural roots rather than those founded in Spanish colonialism. Authors Felipe and Betty Ann Korzenny (2005) concur by stating, ". . . the term *Latino* encompasses almost anyone from a culture with Latin roots." The word "Hispanic" seems to be more accepted by younger generations, while older Latinos view it as a more pejorative term originating from colonization. Women, however, respond more favorably to "Latina" according to editor of *Latina Magazine*, Sylvia Martínez (Granados, 2000). Maria E. Martin, executive director of *Latino USA*, a radio news journal broadcast on NPR, states that her views regarding the term "Hispanic" have shifted somewhat but adds, "My (previous) reaction to the term was that it was the dominant culture's attempt to homogenize Latinos." Martínez feels similarly in that, given a choice, people would not choose either. "Most people think of themselves as Mexican American, Chicanos, Puerto Ricans, Cuban Americans" (Hede, 2009).

Bonnie Davis (2009) presents an extensive look at the complicated issue of racial identity in her latest book, *The Biracial and Multiracial Student Experience: A Journey to Racial Literacy*. As more "mixed race" students enter the classroom, educators and school counselors have been presented with the challenge of reexamining the meaning of racial, ethnic, and cultural identity. Biracial and multiracial students, parents, and educators share personal narratives throughout Davis' book, and Davis tells her own compelling story of one educator's journey to racial literacy. These narratives illustrate the diversity within as well as beyond familial identity.

Even how we have come to use the word "culture" is called into question by the American Anthropological Association (American Antrhopological Association, 1998), which states, "cultural behavior is learned, conditioned into infants beginning at birth and always subject to modification. No human is born with a built-in culture or language." Smedley and Smedley (2005) state that what is common to most anthropological conceptions of culture is the contention that culture is external, acquired, and transmissible to others.

Words are powerful. They matter. The words we use in counseling sessions with students and conversations with peers and parents make a first and lasting impression. The words we choose tell far more about us than they elicit from others. Automatically assigning labels (words), even when seemingly factual, also assigns assumptions and disregards a student's individuality and self-concept. Sometimes, even members of the same family have different ideas about identity. I would like to tell you about Carlos.

Carlos's father, a direct and passionate self-identified Puerto Rican man, called to inquire about counseling for his son. He had many questions. Was I male? Was I black? Did I speak Spanish? How old was I? How much experience did I have? None of my answers were the right ones, though it seemed to please him that I was not unsettled by any of them and respectful of all. I could assure him of three attributes: academic training, practical application, and past success. Malgady & Zayas cite these attributes as qualities important to Hispanic families when seeking professional help (2001).

Carlos was the "identified patient," but beneath his disruptive behavior and impertinent attitude was a simple search for an identity of his own rather than a clinical or familial label.

Carlos's birth mother was of Puerto Rican and American heritage; his birth father was Dominican. Carlos had been adopted by a Puerto Rican couple, now citizens of the United States. His adoptive parents saw him as Puerto Rican and expected him to adhere to their very firm family values and discipline. Carlos, however, identified strongly as part of an African American peer group at the county school where he was bussed as part of the protracted desegregation program. This presented a myriad of problems (Vonk, 2001).

While I understood the complexities of this blended family, my task was to help Carlos become more fluid between worlds and to help his parents and teachers honor his self-identity and internal reality.

One day, Carlos explained football to me. I watch football, but I never understand it. Carlos, at thirteen, taught me more in one hour with crayons and butcher block paper than I had ever learned from John Madden. As he talked, Carlos also concluded he was the running back in his family. He described how they would toss him countless balls, expect him to run with them, score touchdowns, and never complain. The problem, however, was that Carlos felt that he belonged on the other team where his quarterback skills were appreciated. The other team thought he fit better with them; he looked like them, he dressed in the same team colors, and they believed he was smart. They thought it was cool he could come up with all the plays. When he did that for the home team, they punished him for being disrespectful, deceptive, and not "knowing his place." Additionally confusing for Carlos was that his teachers wanted him to be somewhere in the middle—smart and capable but never too "mouthy."

Ponterotto, Mendelowitz, and Collabolletta (2008) state that school counselors need to understand the diverse worldviews and value systems that impact a student's context for learning and interaction both in school and at home. They affirm what Carlos innately knew: "While individual expression and assertiveness may be valued and promoted in high school, such behaviors in a traditional collectivist-culture-oriented family could be interpreted as rude and selfish" (Ponterotto, Mendelowitz, & Collabolletta, 2008).

NEW WAYS OF CONSIDERING STUDENT POPULATIONS

Rather than using words such as "race," "ethnicity," or "culture," consider what we really need to know about a student who doesn't look the same as we do or speak in the same manner as the majority of our other students. Identifying heritage, history, geography, circumstance, and affinity will give us far more information and lead to better understanding of where he or she is literally and figuratively "coming from" than deciding he is African American because of skin color or Hispanic because of name.

Therefore, let's discard outdated, limiting, and often prejudicial words and instead consider using

- Heritage and Historic Memory
- Geographic or Regional Origins
- Circumstance and Situation
- Affinity or Relational Bonds

HERITAGE AND HISTORIC MEMORY

There is no doubt the ways in which students and their families self-identify present important implications for school counselors. The goal of shifting our categorical language is certainly not to further annihilate a child's sense of self, but our language is inadequate, and our understanding of the complexities and nuances of "race, "ethnicity," and "culture" is even more so. Ancestry (lineage) and heritage—that which is transmitted from a predecessor (*Merriam-Webster*, 1973)—are perhaps more specific and accurate ways of discovering an individual's family background or structure. Our previous way of categorizing students (by race or ethnicity) would likely limit our understanding and unwittingly lead to stereotyping. Journalist Walter Lippmann (1997) wrote extensively in 1922 about the word and manifestation of "stereotype." Stereotypes are preconceived depictions of a person, group, or society and prove dangerous, especially when used to justify persecution and discrimination.

Discovery of the unseen is often far more important than the obvious. Ayanna and I had worked together for a few months. She was a verbal child but responded especially well to art therapy. These methods gave us insights, though they served more as a bonding exercise. During one particularly poignant session, Ayanna matter-of-factly stated, "I'm glad you're white."

"You are?"

"Yes," she said, working away on her art, an image of the two of us taking a walk.

"Tell me more about why you are glad."

"Because I don't trust black people. My best friend, Molly, is white. I trust her. But I don't trust the other girls. They're always talkin' about me and stuff. Molly's not like that. My doctor is white. My mom says that black people are always talkin' trash about each other. White people don't do that. I can trust you."

"Well, I'm glad you can trust me, but I'm just wondering if the only reason you trust me is because I'm white."

"Well . . . no." I asked if she could tell me other reasons. She could. "You listen. You don't tell me I'm wrong for feeling bad or sad or mad. You do tell me when I need to change my behavior, but you're not mean about it."

I asked if there was anything else. "Oh yeah!" she said. "You're funny and you laugh at my jokes!"

Later, I talked with her mother, who easily admitted Ayanna "got those ideas about black people" from her. She also disclosed that her own mother had instilled those ideas in her. This bias against African Americans came from Ayanna's grandmother, who was Jamaican born. She viewed herself and her family heritage as vastly different from black Americans. The Jamaican heritage in Ayanna's family was virtually unknown to her but mighty in its implications.

"Heritage" is a word often used with pride. Heritage assumes positive legacy left by ancestors and communal traditions gifted by prior generations. For example, among many Native American/American Indian tribes, the importance of community and collaboration are closely held values that promote prosocial interactions and altruism. Inviting Native American/American Indian elders to the classroom to recount stories of tribal empathy and kindness can assist students in building social skills and school community (Turner, Reich, Trotter, & Siewart, 2009).

Historic memory is collective in nature. It is understood as a representation of the past shared by a group or community. Historic memory fosters and defines group identity, explaining where members have come from, who they are, and how they should behave in the present as it relates to the past (Romano, 2009). Romano further suggests that schools play an important role in shaping collective (historic) memory because they are the first places children learn about important historical events, though most textbooks provide a Eurocentric point of view. For some children and their families, this history is either fictional or biased.

Kathy Graves details a valuable example of the meaning of memory in her 2004 doctoral dissertation titled *Resilience and Adaptation Among Alaskan Native Men*. Taking decades old data, Dr. Graves explored the ramifications of historical trauma, involving "the cumulative emotional and psychological wounding both over a life span and across generations resulting from massive group catastrophes (which) continue to affect current generations of Alaskan Native people" (Graves, 2004). Similar consideration should be given to students whose ancestors were victims and/or survivors of mass traumas such as slavery, the Holocaust, or Japanese American internment. Recently, I was humbled to learn about the heritage and historic trauma of a segment of the Louisiana population (Begnaud, 1964). I thought I knew something about Cajun customs because of Mardi Gras and Anne Rice. I can also relate to the perpetual barrage of intellectual disparagements hurled against people of Cajun ancestry because of similar ones heaved upon my own hillbilly kin. Instead, I was ignorant of the cultural assault suffered by the Acadian people who, like American Indians, were stripped of their cultural pride, first language, and identity (LeBlanc, 2010). Learning this expanded my knowledge base, informed my understanding of the rich Acadian culture beyond gumbo and jambalaya, and has made me more considerate of friends, colleagues, and clients who come from southwestern Louisiana parishes.

Christine Sleeter is professor emerita at California State University, Monterey Bay. Professor Sleeter coined the term and developed the *Critical Family History Theory* which places family in a "socio-cultural historical context" (Sleeter, 2008). She describes research of her own family history in an effort to deepen her understanding of historic memory:

> I explored how this process can work as an entrée into historical memory about race, ethnicity, and identify—revealing the ways in which power and privilege have been constructed, the prices people have paid for that, and the ways in which ordinary people have challenged inequities. (Sleeter, 2008)

GEOGRAPHIC OR REGIONAL ORIGINS

Geographic origin tells us about the place one was born, where he has lived, the terrain he has traveled. Geography encompasses country, region, state or province, topography, and population distribution.

Changing schools is difficult for many students. When the change includes disruption from a known environment to a lesser known or unknown one, difficulty is compounded. With mass transit, mass media, and Internet access now being a part of our daily routine, it is easy to assume that moving from one area to another should be a relatively simple thing. It isn't. Lonborg and Bowen (2004) note that there is a "growing body of literature addressing ethical and multicultural issues in school counseling, yet there is relatively little discussion of the challenges associated with rural counseling practices."

My family of origin lives in the Ozark Mountains of southern Missouri. It may be easy to maneuver the narrow winding county roads in the winter in our SUVs, but it is inconceivable for many of my relatives to maneuver the four lanes of Interstate 44 to visit St. Louis. When they do, it feels to them as if they are visiting a foreign land. Much of the Ozarks, like many regions in Appalachia, is isolated within rugged hills and only accessible via locally maintained roadways. Some areas of the desert Southwest or Northern mountain states are similar. Television and Internet reception is intermittent; cable and satellite connections are often unavailable or unaffordable, not only to families but also to rural schools systems (Zacharakis, Devin, & Miller, 2008).

These are only a few of the things we must consider when students arrive in our metropolitan schools from less populated areas of the country. Dialect, dress, and experience may differ greatly. It is easy to assume that students are delayed by intellect instead of by exposure. On the other hand, students who relocate from urban or suburban areas may seem more advanced than their rural classmates. Familiarity does not necessarily mean comprehension, however. Regardless, helping children feel at home and welcome is the priority.

Geographic considerations may skip generations. As with deeply held ancestry, geography can show up in unexpected ways. Customs, idioms, beliefs, and traditions can have strong ties to a family's geographic origins. Salyers and Ritchie (2006) describe the need for Appalachian cultural awareness as a means of enhancing services to a "forgotten people." In many pockets of America, there is a similar need to recognize difference and distinction based upon geographic location, though many have argued that residents sharing identification with location also share common identity and history (Salyers & Ritchie, 2006).

CIRCUMSTANTIAL CONSIDERATIONS

Circumstantial considerations include societal structures such as economic status, permanence, and access. Examples include students living in poverty, transient (homeless) families, children in foster care or later age adoptions, or a student whose parent is incarcerated, indefinitely hospitalized, or otherwise incapacitated.

The 2005–2007 U.S. Census data estimated that 18.3% of children under 18 years old lived below the poverty level (U.S. Census Bureau, 2009). Children living in poverty present a profound challenge to educators and counseling professionals. Children living in poverty are more likely to report increased levels of anxiety, depression, more behavioral disturbance, and lower level of school engagement leading to a greater incidence of tardiness, absenteeism, and dropout (Amatea & West-Olatunji, 2007).

In 2003, children under 18 accounted for 39% of the homeless population (National Coalition for the Homeless, 2007). Consider the simple ramifications of these facts: every time a child has to change schools, his or her education is disrupted, some estimates speculating as much as three to six months of education being lost with each move, and one study found that 23% of homeless children repeated a grade (National Coalition for the Homeless, 2008). Clean clothes and bathing are luxuries when there is no washer or money for a Laundromat; it is not easy to find homework when there is no safe place to keep it; if a child hasn't had a good night's sleep or is hungry, it is impossible for him or her to concentrate in class. School attendance is especially important for children who are homeless because it may provide one constant in an uncertain world; however, district requirements may make it impractical for children to be registered properly or access transportation. Difficulties in obtaining birth certificates, prior school records, or proof of current residency are typically problematic (Strawser, Markos, Yamaguchi, & Higgis, 2000).

In the instance of later age adoption—that is, adoption after a child is of school age—not only is a student adjusting to a new school, but he or she may be adjusting to a new family, home, and lifestyle. Many later adoptions occur after a child has been living in a residential group home or treatment setting. This, compounded with the original reasons children are available for adoption, raise very multifaceted and often unanswerable questions.

Students whose parent is indefinitely hospitalized or incarcerated often face an assortment of issues such as grief, confusion, and isolation; in both circumstances, they may feel shame. Separation anxiety and attachment issues are prevalent.

The stigma of having a parent in prison can be overwhelming. It is estimated that 1.5 to 2 million children are affected, and the number of children with parents in the correctional system has doubled since 1991 (Miller, 2006). Parent-teacher conferences must be managed in creative ways because incarceration does not always mean the parent has lost rights or legal custody.

Chris and Tony originally came into counseling with their mother. Ms. Simmons had been sentenced to five years in prison for a drug-related felony. She was getting her affairs in order. She was very clear that she wanted her sons to have someone to talk with while she was gone, and her family would not be helpful. The boys, 14 and 15 at the time, were reluctant to talk about how their mother's upcoming incarceration would affect them. It was not until Ms. Simmons was imprisoned that they began to express feelings of embarrassment and fear but also of pride in how their mother was taking responsibility for her actions. Prior to her incarceration, the boys had both been below average students. After she went away, they both worked hard to "make her proud."

This newfound academic success was a surprise to many of the teachers, and they remained baffled as Ms. Simmons had also instructed that no one other than the counselor and the administration be told the reason for her absence. She remained in constant contact with her sons and when possible, conducted parent-teacher conferences over the phone. She was granted early release for good behavior yet missed Tony's graduation. One of the ways in which Chris compensated for the absence of his mother was to become interested in filmmaking. He took as many multimedia classes as he could and documented the daily lives of his brother and himself. He made a special video of Tony's graduation day and sent it to their mother.

AFFINITY OR RELATIONAL BONDS

Affinity or relational bonds may be by choice rather than circumstance, yet there may be an entrenchment in the mores and customs of the group which require consideration. Military families currently present a noble though challenging array of considerations. Conversely, students who belong to gangs or are children or siblings of gang members may feel the same fierce loyalty to their unit, but we as professionals use our skills to counsel them out of harm's way rather than honoring the service of their family member. For some children, this seems unfair; war is war.

Issues common to most all affinity or relational bonds are a strong sense of allegiance, some measure of uniformity, an actual or implied code of honor, and a suspicion of outsiders—those who are not part of the group or faction (Anderson, 1996).

Gang membership almost always carries a negative connotation, but gangs do serve a purpose. A sense of belonging, self-identity, status and emotional support, peer group respect, and sense of security are basic developmental needs which can be acquired for some young people through participation in gangs. Values such as loyalty, responsibility, and group conformity are learned on the streets when they are not available at home (Omizo, Omizo, & Honda, 1997).

In some instances, home is where gang membership begins. In one study conducted, a 14-year-old girl confirmed being born into the gang. "My mother and step-father were leaders in the gang, and I was always there. For my first birthday, I got a tattoo on my arm. . . . I'll be one of them 'til I die" (Molidor, 1996). Molidor goes on to report that the experiences of her sample of female gang members were more like that of a "combat zone than a learning environment." The majority carried a knife to school on a daily basis and had easy access to firearms. Two themes emerged from the study: belonging and power (Molidor, 1996). This is not so different from the reasons young men and women join other, more socially acceptable armed forces.

The current military involvement in the Middle East has presented school counselors with new dilemmas. In school districts located near military bases, it is somewhat easier to establish routine ways of responding to student concerns and crisis. Burnham and Hooper (2008) also find significant age and gender difference in school children's response to the war in Iraq. Girls and younger children report the highest level of fear. Boys may experience war-related fears, but they are less open about expressing them. Younger boys may present as "enamored and excited," while girls present as "worried and troubled" (Burnham & Hooper, 2008). Gathering the facts from parents before addressing the concerns of children is important, as children often fear most what they don't know and may imagine a scenario based on their fears rather than actuality. Somatic complaints may increase with stress. Honest and age appropriate information helps to comfort children. To offset helplessness, emphasize the things students have control over such as school performance and helping out at home (Uniformed Services University of the Health Sciences, 2008).

CULTURAL CONSIDERATIONS

At the end of most chapters, the reader is offered an itemized list of Cultural Competencies and Supportive Strategies. Each competency is followed by the relative ASCA National Model Standards for school counselors. Refer to the *ASCA National Model: A Framework for School Counseling Programs* (American School Counselor Association, 2005) for elaboration.

- Listen carefully; ask questions; do not assume. (ASCA National Model Standards—A.1.a., b., c., A.3. a., b., B.1.a. b., E.1.a., b., c., E.2.a., b., c., d.)

- Research what your students share with you and ask them more questions. (ASCA National Model Standards—B.1.d., B.2.d., C.1.c., D.2.a., b.)

- Construct a consistent climate of inclusion and interest within the school community. (ASCA National Model Standards—A.3.b., E.1.a., b., c., E.2.a., b., c., d.)

- Be proactive in enforcement of consequences for exclusion, prejudicial talk, or behavior without creating backlash. (ASCA National Model Standards—E.1.a., b., c., E.2.a., b., c., d., F.1.a., b., d.)

- Gently, yet persistently, respond to bigotry or intolerance of other school professionals. (ASCA National Model Standards—E.2.a., b., c., d., F.1.a., b., d., F.2.b., c., G.1., 2., 3., 4.)

- Seek other professionals who may have more personal or professional experience with a particular population. (ASCA National Model Standards—D.1.c., E.1.c., E.2.d., F.2.a., G.1.)

- Attend professional workshops, presentations, and conferences to expand cultural and awareness and competency. (ASCA National Model Standards—E.1.c., E.2.d., G.1., 2., 3., 4.)

- Continue to listen, ask questions, and share what you've learned from your students about heritage, geography, circumstance, and relationships. (ASCA National Model Standards—A.1.a., b., c., d., F.1.c., E.2.b., d., F.2.b.)

- Find a container and some colorful index cards. Each day, write something you've learned about "culture" and put it in the container. (ASCA National Model Standards—E.1.b., E.2.d.)

- When your container is full, pass it on to a less experienced colleague. (ASCA National Model Standards—F.2.b., c.)

- Begin filling a new container with gifts of personal and professional growth. (ASCA National Model Standards—E.1.b., c., F.1.c.)

STRATEGIES TO SUPPORT AND FACILITATE CULTURALLY CONSIDERATE COUNSELING

- Invite your students to read, write, and share information about their ancestry and/or heritage. Leave the request open-ended. Do not define the topic for them. Be clear they will not be graded on their acceptance of this invitation.

- Invite your student to make an image of her family doing something together. Invite the student to tell the story of the picture or collage.

- Using a world map, invite your student to point to the places he knows his ancestors have lived. Ask where he (the student) was born. Where would he like to visit to learn more about his heritage?

- Establish a school "Heritage Day." Celebrate ancestry and history through clothing, food, music, and storytelling. Honor elders and others by including stories of family sacrifice.

- Ask your students the following question: *What is worth fighting for?* Then invite him or her to name *four people who would stand beside you in that fight*.

- Be prepared to answer the same questions.

CHAPTER SUMMARY

This is in no way a complete compilation of material regarding populations generally categorized by race, ethnicity, and culture, but it is an invitation to listen, learn, and consider new and perhaps more precise delineations. In future chapters, we will consider the individualized needs of other student populations and provide suggestions for continued professional growth and skill building. Chapters will undoubtedly intertwine. Chapter 2, for example, will explore student religious and spiritual affiliations. Be conscious of the information in Chapter 1 regarding the importance of heritage, history, and affinity. These factors—these considerations—are significant within religious and spiritual identities as well.

2

Religion and Spirituality

A dear friend of mine is a librarian in a rural community. One of our greatest debates has come from his decision to "misplace" a series of children's books asserting dinosaurs were among the species Noah carried to safety upon the ark. My friend would ordinarily dismiss this with a scoff, but he is actually outraged because the series is coded in the Dewey decimal system as "nonfiction." He feels strongly children should not be given false information as fact. I agree with him, though I tend to think there are many things taught as fact which should, at best, be presented as fable. I am not sure where I would store all the books I would like to "misplace." Moreover, I do not want *Free to Be a Family* (Cerf, 1987) or *Heather Has Two Mommies* (Newman & Sousa, 2000) to be misplaced—they are hard enough to find as it is.

My friend is in many ways an open-minded individual, yet this is his blind spot. He cannot bring himself to view these books through an equity lens. To do so would defy his fundamental belief in science and evolution and affronts his personal knowledge base which in turn informs his professional code of ethics. This is a very slippery slope. Rather than allowing children access, he has decided to censor what they read because the belief system espoused in these books offends him. I am astounded by this because my friend, a retired journalist, is a fierce advocate of the First Amendment. At the same time, I am reminded that education does not always teach tolerance, nor does educated always mean tolerant.

Religious and spiritual expression is probably the most delicate of all topics to address in schools and communities. In June 2004, a special issue of the *Professional School Counseling Journal* dedicated an entire issue to the topic of spirituality. Introducing the issue, Sink and Richmond (2004) noted that a sizeable gap in the school counseling literature existed prior to its publication. Although the volume defined spirituality as "an overarching notion that reflects a person's attempts to make sense of his or her world," the authors include religions as expressions of "meaning-making that are uniquely personal as well as communal" (Sink & Richmond, 2004). Because students are generally in the business of trying to make meaning of all aspects of life, it should not be surprising that religion and spirituality are among these aspects. Eaude (2003) writes, this "universal search for meaning and identity . . . relates more to [an] individual's place within culture, to values and relationships." Eaude (2003) further observes

> . . . although many areas of children's needs can usefully be separated into discrete areas, the spiritual overlaps with several other domains, including the emotional, the moral, the psychological. . . . At the very least, we need to understand children's spirituality as worthwhile in its own right, rather than an immature . . . version of adult spirituality.

MacDonald (2004) states, ". . . spirituality is a dimension of human diversity that can no longer be overlooked," and asserts spirituality is "at least implicit in the ASCA ethical tenet on diversity," concluding that spiritual issues factor into identity formation for adolescents and for children, making them important developmentally but admitting impediments to the counseling process exist. While public school counselors are understandably sensitive to matters pertaining to separation of church and state, openness to students' religious and spiritual beliefs and practices should not compromise such principles. Perhaps out of fear of litigation, violation of school policies, or belief that conversation of a religious or spiritual nature would breach professional code of ethics, counselors may deflect or redirect discussions; the mental health community has begun to revisit these assumptions (Sink, 2004). As long as proselytizing or recruiting does not occur, addressing issues germane to a student's well-being need not and should not be avoided (MacDonald, 2004).

The First Amendment Center "works to protect First Amendment freedoms through information and education" (First Amendment Center, 2009). In the publication *Finding Common Ground: A First Amendment Guide to Religion in Public Schools*, the center provides answers to important legal and ethical questions (Haynes & Thomas, 2007) such as, "Is it constitutional to teach about religion?" The answer given is a simple *yes*.

So how might we more comprehensively consider religious and spiritual difference when counseling our students or creating a more considerate school environment? Jennifer Holladay is a co-author of *The ABCs of Religion in Schools* (2009), a document published online via the Teaching Tolerance Anti-Bias Classroom. Holladay suggests four simple rules for advancing understanding of religion's impact on societies and fostering religious tolerance: (1) maintain neutrality, (2) keep it academic, (3) teach about faiths behind holidays, and (4) focus on respectful inquiry.

Haynes and Thomas (2007) provide further statements distinguishing between advancement of knowledge and indoctrination:

1. The school's approach to religion is *academic* not *devotional*.

2. The school may strive for student *awareness* of religions but should not press for student *acceptance* of any one religion.

3. The school may sponsor *study* about religion but may not sponsor the *practice* of religion.

4. The school may *expose* students to a diversity of religious views but may not *impose* any particular view.

5. The school may *educate* about religions but may not *promote* or *denigrate* any religion.

6. The school may *inform* about various beliefs but should not seek to *conform* him or her to any particular belief.

In regard to how religious holidays should be treated in the school, Haynes and Thomas caution,

> . . . recognition of and information about such holidays should focus on the origin, history, and generally agreed-upon meaning of the observances . . . if the approach is objective, neither advancing nor inhibiting religion, it can foster . . . understanding and mutual respect within and beyond the local community. (2007)

Warren Nord, director of the University of North Carolina, Chapel Hill, program in Humanities and Human Values, instructs that a central purpose of education is to teach students about the place of religion in history and culture and criterion of religious curriculum or discussion should be on *significance* as it relates to historical events, themes, and literary texts. Nord (2007) further instructs educators to be sensitive to religious ways of understanding these events and themes but also notes that the First Amendment requires neutrality, stating, "In an ideal world this means (a) taking each party seriously, (b) allowing each party to speak for themselves, (c) providing sufficient time and context, (d) pursuing emotional as well as intellectual meaning, and (e) fairness does not require equal time."

There should be no official conclusions, and students should not be required to agree with the educator. Particular sensitivity must be shown to children who come from minority faiths and ethnic backgrounds. Age is important; critical thinking and the ability to confront ambiguity and cultural conflict come with maturity. Some things may be too controversial (Nord, 2007).

In order to best maintain these rules, basic knowledge of specific religions and belief systems is advisable. Unless one is a religious scholar, however, it is implausible to assume any of us will know all there is to know about our own faith, let alone anyone else's.

"The school counselor needs to have both underlying knowledge of the spiritual values of those in the school community and an understanding of how to access appropriate, specific resources (such as leaders from other faiths) in order to develop effective environments," write Lonborg & Bowen (2004). Some rudimentary facts found in the next section may be useful when relating to students.

SPIRITUAL PATHS TO CONSIDER

The tendency to assume that children's spiritual needs are met only with a faith community does not address the reality that the vast majority of children in Western societies may have no such link.

> The pressing issue is whether, and how, we can address the needs of the majority of children outside religious traditions. Given that spirituality is strongly rooted historically in religion and retains very strong association with it, we need new ways of understanding children's spiritual development, drawing on the insights both of religious traditions and of others less obviously associated with current perceptions of spirituality. (Eaude, 2003)

CHRISTIANITY

Approximately 33% of the world's population regard themselves as Christian (Religious Tolerance, 2009). There are endless denominations, subdivisions, beliefs, and practices which fall under the umbrella of Christianity. Christians share a common belief in the uniqueness of Jesus, that he in some way provided for the redemption of humankind by his death, and was himself resurrected from the dead (Hopfe, 1979).

Many Christians are familiar with their own denomination but have never been exposed to diverse beliefs within Christianity. Within each of these denominations, there are countless derivatives with many theological interpretations, often occurring between members of a single congregation (Religious Tolerance, 2009). A glance at any list of denominations provides a sampling of the variance among self-identified Christians and begins to illustrate how easily disputes might arise as to who and what represent "true" Christian values. Three delineations are often made: *fundamentalist, mainline,* and *liberal.*

According to the Ontario Consultants on Religious Tolerance, fundamentalists and/or evangelical Christians regard being "saved" as necessary for a genuine relationship with God and believe in a literal Bible. Mainline Christians tend to be more inclusive, accepting anyone who follows the teachings of and about Jesus Christ. So-called liberal Christians may follow the teaching of Jesus but may take a pluralistic approach to other religious and/or spiritual viewpoints (Religious Tolerance, 2009).

There are many faiths that fall somewhere in between as shown in Danielle's story.

Danielle had been placed in foster care with her grandparents after being removed from her mother's home because of physical abuse. Danielle preferred this to being placed in foster care with strangers, and she enjoyed the benefits of the financial stability her grandparents could provide, but she began to complain she was never allowed to attend school functions or have friends over. In talking with Danielle's grandparents, what appeared to be isolation was actually seen as protection of Danielle according to the family's religious beliefs. Danielle was not allowed to participate in many school activities because they violated the basic beliefs of Jehovah's Witnesses.

In a booklet for educators, the Watchtower Bible and Tract Society states, "Jehovah's Witnesses feel that their children are better served when parents cooperate with educators, taking an active, helpful interest in their children's education" (Watch Tower Bible and Tract Society of Britain, 1995). Jehovah's Witnesses believe "religious education" is the responsibility of the parents. They have no objection to attendance of general school assemblies or activities as long as it does not interfere with or contradict the beliefs of the family. At the core of these beliefs is all honors should be paid only to God.

School personnel should be aware that Jehovah's Witnesses do not salute a national flag or stand during the national anthem. They do not take part in political activities such as voting. General charitable activities are allowed as long as they do not promote religious holidays or war. Festivals or celebration of holidays such as Christmas and Easter are not permitted, nor do Jehovah's Witnesses recognize birthdays or secular anniversaries such as Mother's Day or Father's Day.

In Danielle's case, she was unable to attend birthday parties or school sporting events and began to feel like an outsider. While her mother was also a Jehovah's Witness, she had not practiced her faith as strictly as Danielle's grandparents. Danielle knew the basic principles but had never felt the full effect of them. As she moved into adolescence, peers, dating, and being a part of the "crowd" was also becoming more important. Danielle was having a difficult time balancing her need for independence with her need for a stable home and caring family.

As a counselor who is not a Jehovah's Witness, I needed to do as much research as possible. I read a few books and articles, but the most beneficial material came from Danielle's grandparents. They brought in material such as the *Watchtower* magazine and gave me a copy of *Questions Young People Ask* (Watch Tower Bible and Tract Society, 1989) which contained chapters on school and morals. In previous positions,

I had child clients whose families were Jehovah's Witnesses, but they were either not of school age or the children were compliant with religious rules and spiritual boundaries. For Danielle, one had everything to do with the other, and the challenge was to help her feel less lonely while respecting her family's belief system and structure.

Although Danielle remained unsatisfied, she and her grandparents were able to come to some compromises. During family counseling sessions, Danielle listed all of the things she wanted to do. Her grandparents combed over the list, discussed each with Danielle and me, and then decided upon the ones they felt appropriate. Some activities were acceptable, such as being on the basketball team, but Danielle had to agree not to participate in singing the national anthem and to skip games which fell on nights when the family attended Kingdom Hall Meetings. In turn, Danielle's coach needed to be informed of these stipulations and abide by them. One important requirement was that the coach be given a copy of the advanced medical directive already in Danielle's file so no inappropriate measures would be taken in case of injury. (Jehovah's Witnesses have very specific beliefs regarding medical procedures, specifically blood transfusions.) Although she was uncomfortable with making an exception to her attendance rules, the coach agreed to do so for Danielle. She also scheduled a time for the team to meet and discuss the issue. Danielle was pleasantly surprised to find her teammates felt her skills were such an asset; they would rather she play when she could rather than not at all.

Danielle continued to struggle with things like holiday parties and being unable to spend individual time with school friends, but with encouragement, she began to make friends at the Kingdom Hall. Her grandparents made efforts to invite these friends to their home and create alternative opportunities for Danielle to expand her social sphere.

Some Christians feel they are quickly becoming the new minority in America, and that with the recent influx of immigrants with differing religious beliefs, Christian *values* are being *devalued* in an effort to accommodate the interests of other faith groups. Organizations such as the Christian Coalition and Christian Educators Association International promote biblical principles as crucial to the underpinnings of American democracy and public education. The Christian Coalition is "committed to representing the pro-family agenda and educating Americans on the critical issues facing our society . . . [including] efforts to improve education . . ." (Christian Coalition, 2009). The Christian Educators Association International (CEAI) regards itself as the only professional association for Christians who are called to serve in public schools (Christian Educators Association International, 2009b).

Matthew Staver (2005) writes, while educators "may not encourage students to accept Jesus Christ as Lord and Savior, teachers may not try to convince students that Jesus is a fictional character," and that educators are protected by the Constitution as public employees and have religious rights under state and federal employment laws. The CEAI is a leader in promoting the rights of religious persons in public education as well as a "Declaration for Public Education" which includes the precept that "Christian churches need not only provide for the spiritual well-being of children, parents, and educators within their congregations but also need to see their involvement in local public schools as part of the churches' vision" (Christian Educators Association International, 2009a).

JUDAISM

Jewish identity cannot be defined solely in religious terms, but for these purposes, the religion of Judaism is the focus. "The unifying feature . . . is a belief in the oneness of God who works in and through historical events and how has . . . chosen the Jewish people as agents" (Hopfe, 1979). Like Christianity, Judaism is widely divided in belief and practices, though there are three main groups: Orthodox, Reform, and Conservative. The National Jewish Population Survey (Ament, 2000–2001) noted that 10% of all Americans who identify as Jewish consider themselves to be Orthodox, 35% consider themselves to belong to the Reform movement, and 26% identify as Conservative.

Orthodox Judaism adheres to the basic tenets of the Talmud, including strict observance of the Sabbath, keeping kosher food laws, gender segregated synagogues, and speaking Hebrew particularly during worship. Reform Judaism is more popular in the United States and Europe, and while believing in the primary principles of Judaism, people within Reform congregations practice in a wide variety of ways and accept female rabbis (Religious Tolerance, 2009). The Conservative movement arose in the 19th century as a reaction to the extremes of the Reform leaders (Hopfe, 1979). Distinguished by a greater concern with the academic study of Judaic texts, members of Conservative congregations adhere more closely to original Jewish law yet advocate Judaism as a "living spirit which would undergo changes coming by themselves" (Markowitz, 1973). Some sources also recognize Reconstructionists, a more recent liberal movement started as an attempt to unify and revitalize (Religious Tolerance, 2009).

In public schools, information about Judaism is largely derived from curriculum containing accounts of the Holocaust and Hitler's dedication to eradicate Jewish people along with many other groups the Nazi regime deemed undesirable. While this ugly segment of history is extremely important in educating students regarding anti-Semitism, it may in some ways undermine or discount the positive and thriving Jewish history which preceded the Holocaust and survives today. The Anti-Defamation League (ADL) has helped many school districts develop policies which are constitutional and help school staff be both inclusive and sensitive to the beliefs or non-beliefs of all students and staff. Providing the administration with the ADL's 2000 publication *Religion in the Public Schools: Guidelines for a Growing and Changing Phenomenon* may help the school to rethink policies.

The Blessing of a Skinned Knee: Using Jewish Teachings to Raise Self-Reliant Children (2001) is written by Wendy Mogel, PhD, for Jewish parents who find the values of their faith at odds with those of the current culture. It is also a beautiful and lyrically written book which would benefit anyone interested in learning more about Jewish culture, values, and worldview. Another book which provides answers to tough questions is Olitzky, Rosman, and Kasakove's (1993) *When Your Jewish Child Asks Why*. By reading books written for parents of faith, we learn what our child clients learn from their families of origin and are able to normalize different religions and spiritualities as life lessons and values which may be very similar to our own but simply taught somewhat differently.

ISLAM

With the second largest following in the world, Islam is perhaps the most misunderstood and recently maligned religion in the United States today. After September 11, 2001, the FBI reported hate crimes against Muslim people (or people perceived to be Muslim) soared 1600% (Schevitz, 2002). Today, educators are still trying to help students make sense of a changing world (First Amendment Center, 2003).

Islamic principles include the belief in Allah as the sole and sovereign God who may be worshipped by other names. Islam teaches the Oneness of mankind. People are created equal in the Law of God, innocent at birth, with one life to live. How one lives his life determines how he will spend eternal existence on the Day of Judgment. Many messengers were sent by God throughout history to impart Allah's teachings, but some misunderstood and misinterpreted them.

Islam requires the practice of *five pillars* of creed, prayer, fasting, charity, and pilgrimage (Teaching Tolerance, 2001). With the onset of the war in Iraq, the non-Muslim world has begun to learn more about the variations within the Islamic faith, Sunni and Shia specifically, although there is still much confusion about the differences. In brief, the differences between these two main subgroups within Islam initially stemmed largely from political disputes, though over time, these differences have produced a number of varying practices and positions which have come to carry a spiritual significance based primarily upon divine right of leadership. Some common misconceptions about Islam include the following:

- *Muslims worship false idols.* "Allah" is the Arabic name or word for the "One True God." Arabic-speaking Christians use the same word for the "Almighty" (Huda, 2004).
- *Most Muslims are Arabs.* Despite pervasive stereotypes, only 20% of the Muslim world population is Arab (Teaching Tolerance, 2001).

- *Muslims are violent, terrorist extremists, and intolerant of other religions.* Terrorism is not justified under any valid interpretation of the Islamic faith. The Qur'an reminds followers that they are not the only ones who worship God. The overwhelming message is that of peace through faith and justice (Huda, 2004).

Ahmed and Reddy (2007) write that Islam is the fastest growing religion and second most popular in the United States. The public most often identifies American Muslims as immigrants or refugees who have recently migrated from developing nations; however, American Muslims may refer to themselves as "indigenous" Muslims, referring to individuals from African American, European, or Hispanic backgrounds who were born and raised in America and as Americans. The mental health needs of the three subgroups of Muslim students—immigrants, refugees, and indigenous—are quite different (Ahmed & Reddy, 2007) and should be taken into account by school counselors.

Muslim students in public schools are often reluctant to ask for accommodation for required prayers or other religious needs. Jum'ah prayer is an obligation of faith that must be fulfilled each Friday. When required daily prayers fall within the school day, Muslim students need a place to pray. Schools have two alternatives. If a school allows extracurricular clubs, then Muslim students may form a student-led club under the Equal Access Act. They could meet for Jum'ah prayers every Friday if all other extracurricular clubs are allowed to meet during that time. Similarly, when Muslim girls wearing head scarves arrive at school where there is a "no head coverings" policy, they need an exemption on grounds of conscience. The Supreme Court has made clear schools may allow released time to meet the needs of students and parents. School officials may not encourage or discourage participation, and they must allow all religious groups to participate (Haynes, 2004).

HINDUISM

Hopfe (1979) characterizes Hinduism as the oldest, most complex, and most tolerant of religions. The Hindu American Foundation (2009) states that two core beliefs are tolerance and pluralism, respecting differences in belief and religion while accepting those paths as legitimate. Based upon these concepts, Hinduism has never sanctioned proselytization.

As Hinduism allows millions of major and minor gods and infinite views, traces of Hinduism can be found in many other religious beliefs. Largely practiced by people of India, Hinduism is often cultural as well as spiritual. Unlike most major religions, Hinduism has no one identifiable founder, though there have been a number of teachers and leaders in its history. Hinduism is based upon "Vedic" literature comprised of four books, each with four parts: mantras (prayers and hymns), Brahmans (instruction), Aranyakas (contemplative teachings), and Upanishads (philosophies) (Hopfe, 1979).

Implications for school counseling includes understanding the "centrality of community" as a metaphor for understanding Hinduism and tends to conceptualize the individual as inherently part of a social whole. The individualism and competitiveness of Western society may be absent in the Hindu family where members know their position in the social structure from birth. Applying such Western values may result in confusion and have a negative impact on the integrity of the family system according to Hodge (2004) who further states that child rearing is typically child-centered. Rather than being pressured to become autonomous and independent, children are socialized to see themselves as an integral part of a divinely ordered environment. Gratification of the child's desires in conjunction with minimum frustration is felt to be conducive for development. Disciplinary actions such as "time outs" are often perceived as too distancing. Adolescence, at least in the Western sense, does not exist in classical Hinduism. In many instances, it may be more advisable to seek solutions within the context of family and community than to support a teen's struggle for freedom and individuation (Hodge, 2004).

Rajiv Srinivasan (Hindu American Foundation, 2010) writes,

> Like most Indian youth in the United States, I faced the inner conflict between my Indian and American identities. At home, I watched Bollywood movies and prayed to Hindu Deities, but at school, I spoke English, played football, and did whatever I could to emulate a typical American childhood. I felt pulled in two directions: one identity abandoning my Indian heritage, the other neglecting my American way of life. Thus, I went through my most formative years without knowing who I was, nor what I stood for. . . . My family follows Hinduism, which is the world's oldest and the third most practiced religion. . . . As a Hindu American, I've been exposed to other religions throughout my education, most notably Christianity and Judaism. In America, Hinduism has always seemed to blend into the background.

As with other student populations, differentiating between degrees of adherence within the Hindu community is important when assessing how to approach any situation. Recent immigrants may have a stronger adherence to the teachings, while second- and third-generation American-born Hindus may have less, or may surprise the counselor by their reliance upon Hinduism to comport themselves.

Shivi Chandra (Hindu American Foundation, 2010) writes,

> . . . being Hindu American represents access to both the secular and the religious facets of man's most ancient attempt to make sense of the world. In the Hindu religious tradition, this is clearly visible in the Vedas . . . at the core, the philosophy always remained the same: that man is a great and powerful being, that because of

the Godstuff of which his soul is fashioned, he may triumph in any situation, that there is a purpose to life, and that is a beautiful and meaningful purpose.

BUDDHISM

There is nothing in the life and teachings of Buddha (Siddhartha Gautama) to indicate he intended to found a new religion (Hopfe, 1979), yet his teachings came to be regarded by Hindus as a reformation and a basis for many religions in Asia and outside of India. The Buddha traveled and taught, though he didn't teach people about his own "enlightenment." He taught people how to realize enlightenment themselves and that awakening comes through one's own direct experience, not through beliefs and dogmas. Buddha taught to accept no teaching without testing it (O'Brien, 2009).

The focus of Buddhism is on practice rather than belief, and the major outline of Buddhist practice is found in the *Four Nobel Truths* and the *Eightfold Path* (McAuliffe, 2008). The Path is divided into three main sections of wisdom (Right View, Right Intention), ethical conduct (Right Speech, Right Action, and Right Livelihood), and mental discipline (Right Effort, Right Mindfulness, Right Concentration).

Buddhist tradition teaches that the "soul" or "self" does not exist. Instead, a combination of five aggregates—the physical body, feelings, understanding, will, and consciousness—make up the human personality which is bound by an endless cycle of birth, death, and rebirth (Hopfe, 1979). This, however, is different from the mainstream perception of reincarnation. O'Brien (2009) writes, ". . . there are two things most people think they know about Buddhism—that Buddhists believe in reincarnation and that all Buddhists are vegetarian." Teachings on rebirth are considerably different from what most people perceive, meaning more a sense of constant renewal than a literal reincarnation. One metaphor compares this to a tree leaf which withers and falls, a new leaf eventually replacing it (Religious Tolerance, 2009). As to vegetarianism, it is encouraged but not required.

"Karma" is a word few in the West truly understand. Westerners too often think it means "fate" or is some kind of cosmic justice system. "Karma" is a Sanskrit word that means "action." In Buddhism, karma has a more specific meaning, which is *volitional* or *willful* action. The law of karma is a law of cause and effect (O'Brien, 2009).

There are two major schools of Buddhism: Theravada and Mahayana. (Zen Buddhism is a sub-school of Mahayana Buddhism.) The distinctions between the various schools and sub-schools are intricate and complicated. Mahayana is dominant in China, Japan, Taiwan, Tibet, Nepal, Mongolia, Korea, and Vietnam and has gained many followers in India. Theravada is practiced more commonly in Sri Lanka, Thailand, Cambodia, Myanmar, and Laos (O'Brien, 2009).

Buddhist psychologies may provide valuable insight and assistance in understanding and helping student clients whose families practice Buddhism. The practice of mindfulness and mindfulness training assists in developing awareness of the hindrances preventing the mind from experiencing things as they are. Hatred, attachment, pride, and jealousy are examples of the obstacles to mindfulness. Meditation is another facet of Buddhism and Buddhist psychology practice which helps the client focus on the immediate experience and notice what is experienced at each moment (Moodley & West, 2005). These practices are not so disparate from our Western desire for our student clients to be aware of emotions and thoughts which prompt negative behavior.

Other aspects of Buddhist psychology which have particular meaning for becoming culturally considerate are compassion and interconnectedness. Clinically, compassion has two levels: the counselor treats the client with compassion and facilitates the development of compassion within the client. Buddhism and Buddhist psychology places emphasis on the appreciation for the connectedness of all living beings and is both humbling and empowering. By developing this appreciation, Buddhist psychology practice teaches that the treatment of oneself affects all other beings because of this interconnectedness (Moodley & West, 2005).

AMERICAN INDIAN, ALASKAN NATIVE, AND PACIFIC ISLANDERS

Even in 1979, Hopfe noted the prudence in describing characteristics found in most American Indian, Alaskan Native, and Pacific Island traditions rather than attempt to outline the specific beliefs and religions of individual tribal affiliations. Attempting to synopsize this vast and eclectic populace is a precarious proposition. Some general characteristics are put forth by Doak (1997), who also notes that "the diversity of American Indian tribes precludes a comprehensive examination of their religions and their belief systems." Doak (1997) does seem to agree with Hopfe (1979) that there are some common tendencies:

- No distinction is made between the animate and inanimate world (animism) in which nature and the elements are central and revered. Local terrain and natural objects are imbued with sacred meaning.
- Ceremonies play an essential role, though rather than for worship as in many religions, Native Americans make no distinction between myth and ritual. Ceremonies and rituals, often involving dance, rhythm, fasting, ordeal, and bathing, are a means of renewing the partnership between the human and nature and/or spirit realms, securing the teaching behind them.

- Oral traditions pass history, belief, culture, and ethics to younger generations more often through story rather than by written word.
- "Medicine man" is a term used by early white settlers; however, the function of the men and women who serve their communities as healers and/or elders is an important one.

In recent years, a trend toward appropriating American Indian traditions and blending them with "new age" spirituality has caused deep despair and concern. In 1993, Valerie Taliman wrote, ". . . while Native Nations continue to the flight for religious freedom rights, 'new age' hucksters and other exploiters of Indian spirituality run rampant throughout the country. . . ." Taliman (1993) reported on the "Lakota Declaration of War Against Exploiters of Lakota Spirituality" unanimously passed at the Lakota Summit V, an international gathering of United States and Canadian Lakota, Dakota, and Nakota nations. This declaration was intended for those who "persist in exploiting, abusing, and misrepresenting the sacred traditions and spiritual practices of the Lakota people." The declaration also urges the Lakota people to prevent "abuse of our sacred ceremonies by outsiders and certain ones among our people . . . with no regard for the spiritual well-being of the people as a whole."

Orrin Lewis (2007) cautions anyone who wants to learn about American Indian religion to read books by American Indian authors, but goes on to say, if someone is trying to learn because they want to become part of it, they face a problem. "American Indian spirituality is not evangelistic. It is private and entirely cultural. You cannot convert to 'Native American' anymore than you can convert to . . . Korean" (Lewis O., 2007).

At the same time, many younger Indians are returning to the spiritual beliefs of their ancestors and reclaiming a culture that was nearly eliminated (Robertson & Gunderson, 2003). As they do so, schools in areas populated by American Indian families are adapting curricula to fill achievement gaps. The National Indian Education Association (NIEA) recommends using culturally based education to increase academic achievement and graduation rates. Citing several research studies which included Alaskan Native, Hawaiian, and Navajo students, NIEA states that culturally based education is more than teaching language and culture. It is a systematic approach fully incorporating and integrating specific cultural ways of thinking, learning, and problem solving into educational practice (Venegas, 2008).

Dr. Joseph Martin (2003) echoes these findings. He stresses that the most successful teachers of American Indian students are those who "teach within the culture, not *about* the culture." Martin elaborates by asserting that these educators succeed with the help of students who act as mediators between the teacher and the Indian peer group, creating an "intercultural classroom," the hallmark of which is dialogue between teacher and students.

Dr. Martin notes a distinct difference in the learning style of American Indian learners (specifically Navajo) versus that of Anglo learners:

American Indian Learners	Anglo Learners
Observe	Act
↓	↓
Think	Question
↓	↓
Act	Think
↓	↓

This preferred learning style of American Indian children—observe first, think about the learning, then take action or practice a new skill—would seem to be applicable to other non-Anglo, non-Western, and/or non-Eurocentric student populations.

PAGANS, WICCA, AND SHAMANISM

It is easy to pour all earth-based belief systems into one big cauldron and be alarmed by them. The unknown or unfamiliar can be unsettling.

Jasper began having bad dreams shortly after he started kindergarten. He would either sleep fitfully, or he would lie awake all night, afraid nightmares would come if he went to sleep. He would then either be late to school or fall asleep in class. He was referred to the school counselor to talk about his declining school performance.

It took a few weeks, but Jasper began to draw pictures during the counseling sessions. They were often dark with stick figures standing in a circle around another smaller red circle. In a few of the pictures, an animal-like head with big ears was hovering above the other figures. Jasper's counselor became very concerned. She had been to seminars on "satanic ritual abuse" and recognized some patterns the presenters had discussed. She was unsure of how to proceed, and as a Christian, she was also frightened. She called a colleague and asked for peer supervision. The colleague, an unflappable older woman, suggested she simply ask Jasper to tell the story of his pictures.

Jasper was a bit hesitant but began by saying, "Well, this is where we say our prayers."

"Who all is there?" the counselor asked.

"Raven and Willow and Sam and Aunt Julie and Mommy," Jasper answered. "Some other people I don't know are there, too."

"Are you there?"

Jasper looked puzzled. "Well, yes and no," he said.

"What do you mean?" the counselor was puzzled as well.

"Well, Mommy says I'm too young to be in the circle. She says I can decide that for myself later. But I'm there in spirit. See?" He pointed to the small reddish image in the middle of the larger circle of stick people.

The counselor was starting to become even more concerned. She had read about dissociative identity disorder. "Tell me about this part of the picture," she said, indicating the animal head in the corner.

"That's Spot," Jasper said, then began to cry.

"Tell me about Spot, Jasper."

"Spot is my dog. He got hit by a car right in front of our house the day I started school." By this time, Jasper was sobbing. The counselor waited. While she was still confused, her instincts were beginning to tell her that Jasper's troubles might not be as unusual as she had imagined.

When Jasper had calmed down some, she asked, "Can you tell me why Spot is here?"

"Well, Mommy and Aunt Julie and Raven and the others are asking him to watch over me. See?" he again pointed to the red part of the artwork. "Mommy takes my Jasper rock with her, and they all say prayers so I won't be so sad and I'll sleep better."

"Does it help you feel better?" the counselor asked, now more intrigued than worried.

"Well, sometimes I feel better when I'm home, but I worry when I'm at school."

"Why is that?"

"Because I'm afraid to let Spot come with me to school. Dogs aren't allowed," Jasper explained. "It's my fault he had to cross the rainbow bridge."

The school counselor decided it was time to talk with Jasper's mother about his dilemma. When she did, Jasper's artwork and his dreams began to make perfect sense. Even though his mother was a bit cautious at first, she told the counselor she belonged to a small group of people who honored the earth in various ways and came together for healing purposes. The "Jasper rock" was exactly that—a large piece of the semiprecious stone, jasper, which represented her son. Spot was a large Dalmatian the family had adopted when Jasper was still in diapers. The dog had followed him everywhere, and though they had tried to keep him from following Jasper to the school bus, he had gotten out and ran after the bus. He was hit by an oncoming car and died instantly. Jasper blamed himself.

The "Rainbow Bridge" was a story about the place animal "allies" go when they die. In many earth-based belief systems, allies are available in this world and beyond to protect and give strength to their human counterparts. Jasper was comforted by the story but was having trouble reconciling his two worlds.

The solution came from the school counselor who was able to broaden her knowledge base and accept Jasper's belief in and need for a calming spiritual companion. During their next session, the counselor suggested Jasper allow Spot to come with him to school the next day.

"But it's against the rules," Jasper said.

"Well, I think we can make an exception, Jasper," the counselor said. "Besides, Spot isn't just any dog. He's your ally, and he has a job to do. There's just one thing. Not everyone has an ally like Spot. It might be best if we kept it private he is coming to school with you."

Jasper's mood immediately lifted. Within a month, he was sleeping soundly at night and his attention and school performance improved. His artwork shifted as well. Rather than drawing nighttime pictures of his mother's prayer circle, he began to draw pictures of himself and Spot at school. While his school counselor was never fully comfortable with his family's beliefs, she did recognize Jasper's need to use his faith to heal from a terrible loss.

This vignette illustrates only one of many paths taken by those whose religious and spiritual beliefs are based on a reverence for nature and observance of seasonal cycles and elemental symbols. Paganism, Wicca, and shamanism are among them. These terms may overlap, but they are not interchangeable; practitioners themselves may disagree about the meanings of the terms (Yardley, 2008).

Paganism encompasses a wide variety of factions who share a common veneration of the Earth and ancient beliefs and traditions of pre-Christian groups such as Druids, Celts, Norse tribes, Greeks, and Eastern European Gypsy Clans (BBC, 2009b). Nature is sacred; the divine is both male and female; nature is composed of four spiritual elements of earth, air, fire, and water, and individuals can create change in their lives by practicing magic through focusing intention and energy toward goals through the use of symbolic rituals (Yardley, 2008).

Wiccan followers may base their beliefs on Earth-centered and/or Pagan principles but focus on the feminine aspect of a higher power or Goddess at least in equity to a masculine interpretation of "God." Respect and protection of the environment often as "Earth Mother" is also often central to Wiccan beliefs (Ontario Consultants on Relgious Tolerance, 2009a).

Emerging research indicates that adolescents are turning more and more to Pagan and Wiccan religions for solace and as a denunciation of what they perceive to be autocratic, paternalistic, and homophobic mainstream religions (Ontario Consultants on Relgious Tolerance, 2009a). Teenage girls are especially drawn to Wicca as a means of embracing their femininity and rejecting sexism. Christine Jarvis (2008) outlines examples of contemporary teen fiction that promote this trend, suggesting these books allow girls to "feel positive about their bodies and sexuality and acknowledge the complex moral decisions many young people face."

Shamanism is not a religion or a spiritual practice as much as a structure within many belief systems practice. Made accessible first by the religious scholar Mircea Eliade (2004), and more recently by anthropologist

Michael Harner (1990), shamanism attempts to collect the commonalities of all basic religions and spiritual practices into a framework of ancestral or cultural meaning.

As in Jasper's case, Earth-centered spirituality is often mistaken for "Satanism" or "devil worship" when in the majority of instances, the existence of an "evil" deity is not acknowledged. Pagans, Wiccans, or those following a shamanic path do not practice "black magic," do not believe in harming humans or animals (i.e., sacrifice), and are not sexual "deviants" as popularly portrayed (BBC, 2009a; Ontario Consultants on Relgious Tolerance, 2009a).

Yardley (2008) recognizes perceptions of teenagers becoming involved in witchcraft or other "alternative" religions as a form of rebellion are pervasive, and although this may be true for some youths, it is also important to remember interests in religious and spiritual pursuits are a natural part of adolescent development. As with other religious practice, teens might take up earth-based spirituality and then drop it after a time. Citing Erickson, Yardley goes on to state that adolescence should be viewed as a moratorium or grace period in which a teen is not fully committed to one identity as "the young individual may feel deeply committed and may learn only much later that what he took so seriously was only a period of transition."

AGNOSTICISM AND ATHEISM

It is difficult for some of us not to think of the infamous Madeline Murray O'Hare when the word "Atheist" is presented (Le Beau, 2005). Murray O'Hare may be seen as a political activist, advocating the belief *not* to believe. While that was certainly her right under the Constitution, her zealous defense was often as vehement as any religious fundamentalist.

Atheism is the absence of belief in any divine or spiritual being. People are Atheists for a number of reasons, including insufficient evidence to support any religion, belief that religion has no relevance in their lives, and disdain of harm done in the name of religion (BBC, 2009a).

Agnosticism is a concept rather than religion and may be understood best by a basic question of whether there is a God and a broad range of answers. The one principle linking all meanings of "Agnostic" is that the existence of God can neither be proven nor disproved, as there is no "evidence" to further either conclusion (Ontario Consultants on Religious Tolerance, 2009b).

In a report co-sponsored by the First Amendment Center (2003) and the Pew Forum on Religion and Public Life, Mynga Futrell is quoted as saying, "Atheism is the deepest difference of all." Futrell works with a Sacramento-based organization, Objectivity, Accuracy, and Balance in Teaching About Religion. "It's a real cultural taboo, such that many people feel it's ok to be prejudiced against atheists," Futrell states. Even the concept of being nonreligious is troubling to many. When the word "religion" is used, those who are not religious are excluded. Mary Ellen Sikes, associate director of the Institute for Humanistic Studies, cautions against the easy use of the word "religion" stating, "Religion is such a broadly used word . . . as if we have shared understanding of what it means . . . not everyone has a religion" (First Amendment Center, 2003, p. 19).

CULTURAL CONSIDERATIONS

- Normalize difference. (ASCA National Model Standards—A.1.a., b., c., d., B.1.a., b., c., d.)

- Enhance commonality. (ASCA National Model Standards—B.2.a., b., c., d., E.2.a., b., c., d.)

- Learn about customs, rituals, symbols, clothing, and jewelry. Often it is the manifestation of religion that causes confusion and complication. (ASCA National Model Standards—E.2.a., b., c., d., D.1.g.)

- Build a vocabulary. Ask students or their parents to help. (ASCA National Model Standards—A.1.a., b., c., B.1.d., E.2.)

- Develop a clear and concise way of explaining your own spiritual beliefs, whether you share them with anyone or not. (ASCA National Model Standards—E.1.a., b., E.2.c.)

- Be cautious about self-disclosure. Assess carefully how sharing one's own religious or spiritual affiliations, belief system, or Atheism might help or hinder the counseling relationship. (ASCA National Model Standards—A.4.a., E.1.a., F.1.b., c.)

- Explore new resources. Some are listed in the Resources section of this book. (ASCA National Model Standards—E.1.c., E.2.d.)

- Respect the rights of students to not discuss their religious or spiritual beliefs or practices. (ASCA National Model Standards—A.1.a., b., c., d., E.2.a.)

- Support excusing students from any school activity or lesson that is objectionable to them or their parents. Have alternative ideas ready for colleagues and be clear that the student isn't being granted a pass but given another way of earning credit or participating in the lesson. (ASCA National Model Standards—A.1.a., b., c., d., B.1.d, D.1.g., E.2.a.)

STRATEGIES TO SUPPORT AND FACILITATE CULTURALLY CONSIDERATE COUNSELING

- Get your own spiritual house in order. Ask for guidance from your own spiritual advisors.

- Attend services of other faiths. Visit organizations such as Ethical Societies or other nonreligious community groups.

- Join an interfaith discussion group in your community. If there isn't one, start one.

- Encourage your school to initiate monthly historical awareness celebrations rather than specifying religiously based holidays.

- Consider the posters, art, books, and memorabilia in your office. Would any student or colleague be offended or confused by anything prominently displayed?

- Discourage the use of school mascots that either stereotype or honor groups or belief systems (e.g., representations of American Indians, Saints, or Rebels).

- Avoid role-play or re-creations of religious practices or ceremonies. However well intentioned, there is a high risk of misrepresenting, mocking, promoting, or over simplifying religious beliefs.

CHAPTER SUMMARY

David Heller (1986) reflects on complex issues raised by children of all ages in *The Children's God*, a thought-provoking book for anyone interested in how children of many different faiths literally view God. Through interviews, drawings, and letters, children reveal the richness of their imaginations, the clarity with which they see God, and the deeply spiritual questions they have for Him—or her, them, or it.

Susan Lonborg, PhD, is director of the School Counseling Program, and Neal Bowen, PhD, is assistant professor of psychology at Central Washington University, Ellensburg, Washington. They provide recommendations in summary of their own work in the area of "Counselors, Communities, and Spirituality: Ethical and Multicultural Considerations" (Lonborg & Bowen, 2004). School counselors should anticipate the ethical challenges associated with their highly visible lives, especially in rural or other small communities or districts. Counselors should identify and be prepared to use a decision-making model when confronted with questions of competence. Counselors need to be familiar with community norms and values in order to thoughtfully consider the impact their own personal and professional behavior may have on the school as well as current and future counseling clients. Ethical school counseling requires an understanding of one's own worldview, including spirituality, as well as an awareness of the diverse worldviews existing in his or her school community.

3

Different Abilities

Disability is not always designated as part of the diversity spectrum. In the 2003 book *Diversity in Human Interactions: The Tapestry of America*, Leigh and Brice provide concrete examples of accommodations and how they benefit multiple consumer groups, not just those with disabilities. Examining physical, mental, mobile, and cognitive disabilities, they cite research which indicates psychotherapists and/or counselors who have even a small amount of training in disability-related issues "reveal significantly less bias in case conceptualization and treatment themes" (p. 182). Leigh and Brice discuss issues of disability culture to which parents and educators most likely do not belong nor understand. They advocate confronting our own stereotypes and the meaning of the work in order to examine personal beliefs and professional behaviors.

For centuries, people with disabilities were thought to be helpless, indigent, and were often forced into institutions and asylums without equal opportunities or protection. The disability rights movement of the 1960s led to a number of victories, including the Education for all Handicapped Children Act and the Americans with Disabilities Act in 1990 (Office of Special Education and Rehabilitative Services, 2004).

The Individuals with Disabilities Education Act (IDEA) provides financial assistance to state and local education agencies for special education and related services to eligible children between the ages of 3 and 21 (Henderson, 2009). Categories of disabilities under IDEA include autism, deafness, deaf-blindness, hearing impairments, mental retardation, multiple disabilities, orthopedic impairments, other health impairments, severe emotional disturbance, specific learning disabilities, speech or language impairments, traumatic brain injury, and visual impairment.

IDEA requires states to ensure the provision of full educational opportunity to all children with disabilities. Related services are provided if students require them in order to benefit from specially designed instruction. IDEA instituted the development of Individualized Education Programs (IEPs) or plans with specific content and a required number of specific participants at an IEP meeting. IDEA also requires written notice to parents regarding identification, evaluation, and/or placement and requires reevaluations be conducted at least every three years.

IDEA delineates specific requirements for local education agencies to provide impartial hearings for parents who disagree with the identification, evaluation, or placement of a child.

According to the Developmental Disabilities Act, section 102(8) (Office of Special Education and Rehabilitative Services, 2004), the term "developmental disability" means a severe, chronic disability of an individual five years of age or older who is

1. attributable to a mental or physical impairment or combination of mental and physical impairments;

2. manifested before the individual attains age 22;

3. likely to continue indefinitely;

4. results in substantial functional limitations in three or more of the following areas of major life activity:

   a. self-care,
   b. receptive and expressive language,
   c. learning,
   d. mobility,
   e. self-direction,
   f. capacity for independent living,
   g. economic self-sufficiency; and

5. reflects the individual's need for a combination and sequence of special, interdisciplinary, or generic services, supports, or other assistance that is of lifelong or extended duration and is individually planned and coordinated, except that such term, when applied to infants and young children, means individuals from birth to age five, inclusive, who have substantial developmental delay or specific congenital or acquired conditions with a high probability of resulting in developmental disabilities if services are not provided.

People with disabilities make up one-fifth of the United States, representing the largest single demographic group. Despite this fact, the disability community continues to face challenges of invisibility, architectural barriers, and discrimination. Historically, disabilities have been cast in a negative light, the individual often depersonalized through terms such as "patient" or "subject."

Smart and Smart (2006) identify distinct models of disability and their implications for the counseling profession. The Biomedical Model of disability is the most well-known. Rooted in the scientific method, this model is backed by the medical establishment and defines disability in the language of science and medicine as a problematic condition to be treated on an individual basis. The biomedical model assumes pathology is present, objectifying persons as having defects, deficiencies, dysfunctions, or abnormalities. Bickenbach (1993) states, "The essence of disablement, in this view, is that there are things *wrong* with people with disabilities." The biomedical model seldom leaves room for issues of environment, interaction, or social justice.

The Functional and Environmental models of disability are both interactional models (Smart & Smart, 2006). Disability is defined in relation to the skills, abilities, and achievements of the individual in addition to biological or organic factors. In these models, the definition of disability, the causal attribution, and the solution are not found wholly within the individual but recognize the importance of environment along with biology. Environment is thought to exaggerate or in some instances, even create conditions or situations leading to disabilities.

The Sociopolitical Model, sometimes referred to as the Minority Model of Disability, is a more recently developed model. This model refuses to accept the inferior, dependent, and stigmatizing definitions of disabilities; instead, disability is seen as a social construct in which (a) people with disabilities must define disability, (b) experts or professionals must not be allowed to define disability or determine outcomes for people with disabilities, (c) deviance or pathology is rejected as causal.

The delineation of models also underscores the issue of language when discussing disability issues, rights, and school counseling concerns. The disability community and advocates have attempted to reassign meaning to the terminology used to describe disability and disabled people. In the United Kingdom, for example, the term "disabled" is used by people within the disability rights movement to denote someone who is "disabled by society's inability to accommodate all of its inhabitants." This "reassignment of meaning" (S. Linton, 1998) has shone light on the ongoing *ableism*, which has reinforced the dominant culture's view of those who are determined to be disabled. In addition, specific cultures have specific views of disability and services to individuals with disabilities (Stone, 2005).

While I ordinarily use the terms "challenged" or "differences" rather than "disabled" or "disabilities," I accept Linton's (1998) assertion that although they may be well-meaning, they can also be cumbersome and convey paternalistic "do-goodery." I have seen a shift in recent years. People with disabilities are reclaiming the word "disabled" much as other groups have reclaimed identity labels. The Person First Movement asks people to use "Person First Language." Rather than a "blind student," by using the phrase "a student who is blind," the goal is to remove objectification. Some people with disabilities support the Person First Movement while others do not. As with all student clients, the best practice is to ask how he or she refers to him- or herself. With that said, I present the following material in the words I have come to use most often. From my perspective as an advocate and as an agent of change, these words leave open fewer possibilities for bias.

PHYSICAL LIMITATIONS

Just as there are many perspectives on models of disability, there are many different ways in which disabilities are categorized. Physical limitations cover a broad range of both congenital and acquired conditions. Congenital conditions are those present at birth or shortly thereafter; acquired conditions occur though injury or disease and interrupt childhood development.

According to IDEA, these conditions include orthopedic impairment, brain injury, or other health impairment. By reason of these conditions, students are substantially limited in their ability to take part in routine school activities and need special education and related services (Office of Special Education and Rehabilitative Services, 2004).

While no list seems to include all variables, some conditions affecting students include cerebral palsy, muscular dystrophy, traumatic or acquired brain injury, spinal cord injury, spina bifida, and cystic fibrosis. Other conditions which may be less overt are Tourette's syndrome, epilepsy, asthma, diabetes, and cleft palette. So-called invisible disabilities are conditions causing chronic pain or chronic fatigue such as fibromyalgia, rheumatoid arthritis, immune disorders, Celiac's disease, Crohn's disease, Sickle Cell Anemia, Lupus, or some cancers.

Paralysis and/or amputations may be caused by several different factors, but the effects of mobility are similar if not the same. Visual differences are represented on a continuum of low vision to legal blindness. Hearing impairment is one of the most prevalent disabilities in the United States, ranging from auditory disorders to mild and moderate hearing loss and deafness.

Students who are deaf may or may not belong to the "Deaf" community. Remembering culture is a set of social behaviors, beliefs, history, and unique language, many people identify as members of "Deaf Culture" and need to be understood as such. This view of deafness recognizes that Deaf people often reject the idea they need to be "fixed" or "cured" and are proud of their differences and enjoy the uniqueness of their community (Kluth, 2006).

Sue and Sue (2008) discuss common errors which occur when counseling individuals with disabilities, many of which are errors of omission. A counselor may fail to ask questions about certain aspects of a student client's life due to an assumption that the issue is unimportant or does not exist for the student. For elementary school children, it might be easy to assume he or she was not interested or capable of participating in sports or theater. For teens, issues such as dating or sexuality may be ignored.

DEVELOPMENTAL AND COGNITIVE DIFFERENCES

The term "culturally competent" is defined in the Developmental Disabilities Act as "services, supports, or other assistance that are conducted or provided in a manner that is responsive to the beliefs, interpersonal styles, attitudes, language, and behaviors of individuals who are receiving services and in a manner that has the greatest likelihood of ensuring their maximum participation in the program" (Developmental Disabilities Assistance and Bill of Rights Act, 2000).

Defining developmental and cognitive differences can be difficult. Many have a base in physiological or biological processes within the individual student, such as a genetic disorder or a traumatic brain injury. Others may be based in the chemistry or structure of the child's brain. Levels of functioning can vary greatly. Down syndrome, traumatic or acquired brain injury, and autism are all included in the category of cognitive disabilities but may also have physical ramifications. Mental retardation is diagnosed based on severity from mild to profound according to the *Diagnostic and Statistical Manual of Mental Disorders* (American Psychiatric Association, 2006).

Milsom (2006) states, " . . . professionals who are uncomfortable with individuals who have disabilities might avoid contact with those individuals." She cites Bowen and Glenn (1998) in suggesting that school counselor bias against students with disabilities could result in low expectations for the student client. I confess, this was one of my own biases and clinical limitations—until I was unexpectedly put in a position of providing treatment in residential settings where the majority of clients were challenged by mental retardation.

I never felt an aversion to the clients, but I did feel I was ill equipped to help them. My IQ (intelligence quotient) is fairly high—"smart enough to keep up but not so smart I get lost," I often say to intellectually gifted clients who need to know but don't want their treatment to become a competition. I can be analytical and abstract to the point of being cerebral. I wasn't sure what I would "do" with clients who had developmental and/or intellectual deficits. In short, I did not see these clients as capable of *doing* their own healing work. I was very wrong.

Unencumbered by self-conscious apprehension about counseling, most of the clients took immediate charge of their treatment and embraced me as a capable helper. They often assigned me tasks to help them "get better." The goals were often concrete and behaviorally based. There was little need to process the whys and wherefores, but often when uncomplicated insights were spoken, they were profound and lasting. So were the lessons I learned during that time in my clinical life.

LEARNING DIFFERENCES

Learning differences (disabilities) are neurologically based processing problems which interfere with learning basic academic skills. They can also interfere with organization, planning, and abstract reasoning. Learning differences are unique to the individual student and may appear in a variety of ways making diagnosis difficult. A cursory way of explaining learning differences is a discrepancy between intellectual capability and achievement. Difficulty with input, integration, memory, and output interfere with a child's ability to process information and extrapolate from it.

Learning differences are often thought to fall into four broad categories: spoken language, written language, arithmetic, and reasoning. Formerly termed "Academic Skills Disorders" by the American Psychiatric Association (2006), learning disorders are identified by specific criterion and are specifically delineated. The *Diagnostic and Statistical Manual of Mental Disorders* (fourth edition, text revision), or *DSM-IV-TR*, lists reading disorder, mathematic disorder, and disorder of written expression. Some educational diagnoses such as dyslexia are not identified within the *DSM-IV-TR* but are recognized for special education services.

GIFTED LEARNERS

A learning difference frequently overlooked in the literature is that of gifted, exceptional, or higher ability learners. Peterson (2006) asserts that counseling and related educational programs give little or no attention to the complex emotional and developmental concerns of high ability students. Peterson postulates both educators and counselors may not understand or respond appropriately to these students for a number of reasons, one of which is that "[a]ssociating the words disability or risk . . . with the idea of giftedness may not resonate with educators . . . yet pertinent research and clinical evidence support the idea that counseling approaches when working with gifted [students] should be adjusted to accommodate their abilities and needs . . . as advocated by the American School Counselor Association." It is not uncommon for students with higher abilities to have similar social isolation issues as peers on the other end of the continuum, and a profoundly gifted child may have fewer intellectual peers throughout the country, let alone his or her own school or community. Heavy emphasis on achievement outcomes sometimes lead to the neglect of other important issues such as happiness, well-being, and life satisfaction (Peterson, 2006).

When considering a child for referral to a gifted program, cultural factors often play a role. In one ethnographic study, themes in the language of dominant-culture teachers reflected dominant-culture values as they explained reasons for referrals. Themes of good behavior, verbal assertiveness, perceived work ethic, social status, and social skills reflected the biases of dominant-culture educators. Children from cultures that do not value verbal assertiveness or "standing out," or students with low English proficiency, behavior problems, low socioeconomic status, and poor social skills might preclude proper identification for giftedness (Peterson, 2006).

If children relocate from school to school, they may be viewed in vastly disparate ways depending upon assessment personnel, assessment tools, and school resources. They may also present differently from school to school, depending upon comfort and circumstances of the move. I recall my own confusion when moving from the West Coast where school resources were far greater than those of rural Missouri. I had been placed in accelerated classes since starting school but was considered "behind" when we moved back to the Midwest. This confused not only me but also my parents. It was difficult for them to understand how I could go from straight As in a larger, more demanding school environment to potential Cs in a small country schoolhouse. On the West Coast, I had excelled in "new math" even my mathematically gifted father didn't understand, yet back in Missouri, I struggled with basic multiplication tables.

Thomas and Ray (2006) advocate a systems' perspective when counseling gifted or exceptional students and their families. They note that although systems' perspectives are not traditionally employed in school counseling, they are effective in responding to the needs of students and their families as advocated by the American School Counselor Association National Model. Thomas and Ray cite three helpful family system models, all of which view family systems from a developmental perspective: Belin-Blank Center Model, structural-strategic approach, and an imaginative-postmodern approach. In addition to typical counseling skills, Thomas and Ray suggest those who work with both gifted clients and/or clients with learning or other disabilities should have a solid knowledge of the individual student in a variety of contexts. They write, "At a minimum, understanding the potential benefits of family counseling in relation to disability and giftedness will help school counselors to make appropriate referrals and clearly communicate to students and their families what they might expect from family counseling and how such counseling might help them" (p. 64).

LEARNING THEORIES AND MULTIPLE INTELLIGENCES

Whether we are school counselors, social workers, psychologists, nurses, or educators, we probably had basic exposure to theories of human development and learning, and there are likely nuggets of truth in each of them. Maslow's hierarchy of needs makes sense. If we spend any time at all with children, Piaget's cognitive development stages are difficult to dispute. If we spend time with adolescents, Pavlov and Skinner are unavoidably applicable. Then researchers like Bruner, Kolb, and Gardner came along and made us think.

Howard Gardner (1983) defines intelligence as "the ability to solve a problem or create a product that is valued in a society" (p. 3). In 1983, Gardner proposed an approach to intelligence which suggested there are several different ways to solve a problem. Gardner's theory of multiple intelligences was in sharp contrast to typical, linear theories of intelligence.

In the first chapter of *Frames of Mind: The Theory of Multiple Intelligences,* Gardner (1983) offers a scenario of a young girl asked a series of questions, assessments of her memory and her capacity for abstraction. These questions and tasks are administered in order to measure the girl's IQ, which as Gardner points out, " . . . is likely to exert appreciable effect upon her future, influencing the way in which her teachers think of her and determining her eligibility for certain privileges."

Gardner determined that intelligence was not finite by definition but should be differentiated by predominant type. Our current understanding of diverse learning styles is largely due to Gardner and expanded upon by other scholars. Because of them, we recognize the specific needs of those student clients whose primary style of taking in information falls into the following categories: linguistic (verbal), musical (auditory), spatial (visual), kinesthetic (bodily or physical), mathematic (logical) interpersonal (social), and intrapersonal (solitary).

Frames of Mind is well beyond its tenth printing, and often finds a home on bookshelves of special education teachers, creative arts therapists, and child psychologists and school counselors working with students who clearly do not learn easily in the modern secular school environment. Gardner (1983) spends time delineating types of learning, illustrating how traditional, non-Western learning environments emphasize different intelligences from those of European and North American elementary and secondary schools. However, Gardner has "elected not to pursue" questions such as whether the intelligences are the same in quality or quantity across groups, such as males versus females or ethnic groups. He defers to the work of others such as Carol Gilligan and Stephen Mithen when it comes to *culture considerations.* How children learn is also important in how they learn to change behavior, understand emotion, and integrate interpersonal skills.

COMMUNICATION AND SENSORY CHALLENGES

A communication disorder is impairment in the ability to receive, send, process, and comprehend concepts or verbal, nonverbal, and graphic symbol systems; it may be mild to profound, developmental, or acquired. A communication disorder may result in a primary disability, or it may be secondary to other conditions (American Speech-Launguage-Hearing Association, 1993).

My very mobile family lived in Washington State when I was in the second grade. The public school I attended was probably one of the best in terms of resources, and there I received about six months of speech therapy to help with my inability to make hard consonant sounds. I don't know if I carried a diagnosis, but now I would assume it to be an articulation disorder as defined by the American Speech-Language Hearing Association: the atypical production of speech sounds characterized by substitutions, omissions, additions, or distortions that may interfere with intelligibility. I have many *distinctions*, but my speech has been the most difficult for me to embrace. I hate to be misunderstood—literally and figuratively.

The one and only time I attempted to get out of something based on my distinctions was in college. I could not bear to be videotaped during a required speech class and met with the instructor and the department chair to plead my case. Apparently, I pled too well. Their only compromise was to tell me I didn't have to view it. I often consider going back and sharing with them the irony of my professional choices. Not only do I talk for a living, but I talk in front of large audiences. My frustration with being misunderstood has informed the way in which I work. Not only do I strive to understand my clients, I also strive to be clear. I feel this is especially important with children, and I will say very directly, "I had to learn to talk a bit differently. If you don't quite hear or understand me, please ask me to repeat myself or say it in a different way. It will not bother me or hurt my feelings. I'd rather you ask than to misunderstand." I also ask if I may do the same. This has often become an inadvertent but important transferential moment.

While expressive language disorder, mixed receptive-expressive language disorder, phonological disorder, and stuttering may impact learning, they are considered separate from learning disorders by the psychiatric community. Similarly, pervasive developmental disorders are not categorized by the *DSM-IV-TR* as learning disorders but as autonomous disorders of infancy, childhood, or adolescence. Autistic disorder, Rhett disorder, childhood disintegrative disorder, and Asperger disorder all fall within this spectrum. Attention-deficit and disruptive behavior disorders likewise are separate and include attention-deficit/hyperactivity disorder, conduct disorder, oppositional defiant disorder, and disruptive behavior disorder. Tic disorders encompass Tourette syndrome and transient tic disorder.

Elimination disorders, selective mutism, reactive attachment disorder, and movement disorders can be especially challenging for educators and counselors and generally need to be referred for more specialized and intensive medical and/or psychotherapeutic treatment.

UNIVERSAL DESIGN FOR LEARNING

Universal Design is an approach to designing course instruction, materials, and content to benefit people of all learning styles without adaptation or retrofitting, providing equal access to learning—not just information. Although the design enables students to be self-sufficient, the educator is responsible for imparting knowledge and facilitating the learning process. Although Universal Design benefits students with disabilities and challenges, all student experiences may be enhanced by the "multiple and flexible" principles of presentation, expression, and engagement (Center for Applied Technology, 2010; National Universal Design for Learning Task Force, 2010).

CULTURAL CONSIDERATIONS

- Embrace difference. (ASCA National Model Standards—A.1.a., b., c., d., B.1.a., b., c., d.)

- Enhance strengths. (ASCA National Model Standards—B.2.a., b., c., d., E.2.a., b., c., d.)

- Learn about different abilities, capacities, and communication styles. (ASCA National Model Standards—(D.1.g., E.2.a., b., c., d.)

- Ask students to teach you and their peers about both their challenges and triumphs. (ASCA National Model Standards—A.1.a., b., c., B.1.d., E.2.)

- Be willing to talk about your own physical, developmental, or learning challenges in a clear and boundaried way. (ASCA National Model Standards—E.1.a., b., E.2.c.)

- Explore resources both to enhance your knowledge and also to benefit your student clients. Some are listed in the Resources section of this book. (ASCA National Model Standards—E.1.c., E.2.d.)

- Be sensitive to students if they are not yet willing or able to discuss their differences with peers or others, yet help them recognize your need to know so that you can help better and with less bias. (ASCA National Model Standards—A.1.a., b., c., d., E.2.a.)

- Expect as much from students with differences as you do from others, but make sure they have access and resources to assist in achievement academically, emotionally, and creatively. (ASCA National Model Standards—A.1.a., b., c., d., B.1.d., D.1.g., E.2.a.)
- Be an advocate for schoolwide accessibility. (ASCA National Model Standards—A.1.a., b., c., d., B.1.d., D.1.g., E.2.a.)

STRATEGIES TO SUPPORT AND FACILITATE CULTURALLY CONSIDERATE COUNSELING

- Examine your thoughts, feelings, beliefs, and experiences regarding different abilities. Who are the students with whom you empathize? Who are the students you feel are "using their disability" as an excuse?
- Invite your students by saying, "Tell me about your wheelchair," or "Would you please tell me about your hand?" Thank them for helping you to learn.
- Visit agencies which specialize in services to disabled individuals and residential facilities for adults with both physical and developmental challenges. Ask them about school when they were younger. What helped and what didn't?
- Encourage your school to adopt Universal Design for learning.
- Encourage the use of inclusive literature and media. Become familiar with the books in your school library and make a list of those which include characters with a variety of abilities. Do some research to see if there are others you can suggest to the librarian or English teachers.
- Avoid role-plays which encourage "able" students to "walk a mile in another's shoes." These are common techniques for encouraging empathy, but they often exploit and embarrass children who have differences. Instead, invite the students to explain or show their peers what a regular day is like for them. Invite them to reenact their life or depict a self-portrait. Include all students in this invitation.
- Invite your differently abled students to share with others how they would like to be treated by their peers, teachers, and adjunct staff. What terms do they use to describe themselves? What words or labels do they dislike? What could they use help with? What would they prefer to do on their own?

CHAPTER SUMMARY

In this chapter summary, I defer to Smart and Smart (2006) who concisely outline the following implications for the counseling profession:

1. Counselors should engage in an ongoing examination of clients' feelings about the experience of disability, difference, and/or challenge and the resulting interaction of the counselor's own identity.

2. Counselors should recognize that most individuals with disabilities do not accept the tenets of the Biomedical Model of disability.

3. Counselors should recognize that the disability is simply one part of the individual's identity.

4. Counselors should understand that empowerment for clients with disabilities include values such as attention to health, adaptation, competence, and the enabling environment.

5. As with all clients, counselors need to guard against imposing their values.

6. Power differentials between counselor and a client with disability should be addressed.

7. Counselors should listen to clients and be willing to hear about experiences of prejudice and discrimination.

8. Counselors should recognize that professional training may have been inadequate to prepare them for work with clients with disabilities.

9. Counselors should examine their willingness to broaden their vision about the experience of disability.

10. Both outreach efforts and collaborative learning can be achieved by learning which agencies clients find helpful—or not.

11. When appropriate and possible, counselors should intervene at institutional and political levels.

12. Counselors should recognize that it is necessary to clearly articulate the assumptions about models of disability that underlie research studies.

Teaching children about the contribution of various populations such as specific ethnic groups, women, and even sexual orientation has been recognized as important additions to educational curricula and programs. Disability history, however, has been largely ignored in schools. In 2006, West Virginia led the way in changing this trend by passing an act establishing Disability History Week. Other states such as Florida, North Carolina, Washington, and Idaho have followed. These and other efforts to integrate disability awareness into educational contexts reflect effective youth leadership development, which endeavors to learn about history, values, and societal beliefs. Outcomes include decrease in negative behaviors and increase in positive attitudes, behaviors, self-esteem, problem solving, health decisions, and interpersonal skills. The increase in these activities and skills is linked to increased self-efficacy, goal setting, decision making, and working well with others (Disability History Museum, n.d.).

Milsom (2006) writes, "Successful implementation of any type of programming depends on support from administrators and cooperative efforts from school personnel. . . . Negative messages can unintentionally be communicated to students via language or procedures" (p. 70). Milsom further elaborates by giving examples of schools that single out students with disabilities, rather than acknowledging all students learn differently, might unintentionally communicate those students are less worthy than others. Educators should show high levels of commitment, hope, and optimism so students do not limit their aspirations.

In Chapter 4 of *Culture and Disability* (Stone, 2005), Jezewski and Sotnik present a culturally sensitive model of intervention for addressing the needs of consumers from many backgrounds, which includes understanding of disability, communication, age, cultural competency, time and/or timing, cultural background of the specific client, stigma, power and/or powerlessness, bureaucracy, politics, and networking. This model stresses the importance of adapting programs and services to the individual client and also how different abilities are perceived in their specific culture, community, and belief system.

Chapter 26 of *Counseling the Culturally Diverse: Theory and Practice* (Sue & Sue, 2008) contains a valuable table of "Things to Remember When Interacting With Individuals With Disabilities," which provides clear and simple suggestions for considerately interacting with not only student clients but also colleagues, parents, and others in a variety of settings.

4

Aesthetic Issues

It was always difficult for me to categorize my differences. Recurrent questions—"What happened to you?" or "What's wrong with you?"—served to set me apart but could never elicit an accurate response. Many years later, I discovered if someone had simply asked me to tell about myself, I might have been able to do so. Had anyone gently said, "Please tell me about your scars," I could have explained how they came to be. It is not a question, but an invitation. I have adapted the frame of invitation as a central part of my clinical work.

No child should have to answer the question, "What's wrong with you?" yet we live in a world in which people feel entitled not only to ask but to answer for us if we don't. In pondering how we got here, I only have to turn on the television, radio, or computer. Reality and entertainment TV, the 24-hour cable news cycle, Internet blogs, and social networking have conditioned us to feel that invasion of privacy is our right. Everyone seems to know everything about everyone else and feels entitled to comment upon it. This is hardly considerate.

FEATURES AND PHENOTYPES

Facial features and phenotypes are the visible characteristics of our genetic makeup and environment. Within cultural groups and even within families, there can be broad variations in these characteristics. In *The Biracial and Multicultural Student Experience*, Bonnie Davis (2009) presents poignant personal narratives of student, parents, and educators, which illustrate the conflicts which arise for many people. Skin color and tone, hair texture, facial features, and eye color are among the traits most often misidentified or criticized and by which students are judged by peers and professionals.

In Chapter 10, I tell the story of Jasmine, one of two daughters born to the same mother and father but demonized for having more "black" features than her sister. I also remember Tess, an intern I supervised many years ago. Tess was a statuesque country girl with bright red curls, big green eyes, and milky skin. The sprinkle of freckles across her high cheekbones and her horn-rimmed glasses gave her a smart, wholesome, yet mischievous air. Her smile was infectious.

Tess was always plagued by her hair. She joked that she had to go to the beauty shop in the black area of her hometown to get it done. One day, someone at the beauty shop recognized her. They also asked about her mother, but they were referring to her sister. When she got home, she told her family about the experience, and they decided it was time to tell her the truth about her family. Her "sister" Terry had in fact given birth to her. Her father was Terry's high school boyfriend, an African American baseball player who had left the area to play for a minor league team. Her family worried she would have more problems if the truth was known, so Tess was raised to believe her grandparents were her parents and her birthmother her older sister. Discovering the truth was painful for Tess, but it was also validating. She had never felt quite "right" in her own skin. She had been confused when people made racially charged comments about her hair.

Students who know their heritage have similar experiences and are also bewildered when their natural features are called into question or criticized. I frequently counsel children who feel they are ugly because of specific characteristics. At one time, it was more prevalent among girls. Now these self-image issues seem to plague boys nearly as often. Sara Halprin (1996) wrote a powerful book in which she describes the "magical power of ugliness." She also writes,

> Ugliness, in the eye of the perceiver as in the heart of the one perceived, can be as much of an obstacle to spiritual growth and psychological wholeness. . . . Ugliness as a basic attribute is as much of a challenge as any other difference from mainstream values, such as racial or ethnic difference, poverty, physical handicaps, life-threatening illness, visible scars, extreme old age. More than any of these other values, which have certain sensory-grounded characteristics that can be described with some accuracy, ugliness is entirely a subjective judgment based on a consensus by those who observe, whether they are external judges or internal. (p. 187)

BODY SIZE AND SHAPE

Body image issues, eating disorders, and body dysmorphia were once considered mostly white girls' issues though research is beginning to show less significance between cultural groups as well as gender. Because all girls are inundated with messages regarding the importance of thinness for success in Western culture, no racial or ethnic group is immune to these influences. One study reported that 80% of girls surveyed reported body dissatisfaction while another estimated 10% of individuals in treatment for eating disorders were male (Choate, 2009; Shiltz, 2005) with the latter number rising steadily as more and more boys and men identify body image issues.

Choate (2009) states that successful body image dissatisfaction prevention incorporates two primary strategies: (1) enhancement of protective factors and (2) inclusion of a broad-based, holistic focus. Rather than a "pathology" driven model emphasizing treatment, the most promising programs incorporate factors that build upon strengths, promote resilience, and buffer from the development of body image issue and subsequent eating disorders. School counseling in particular is based upon a comprehensive, development model that emphasizes students' positive resources and strengths and is therefore poised to take the lead in design and implementation of programs that strengthen proactive factors at the individual, family, peer, and school levels.

Choate (2009) identifies five Protective Factors in her Body Image Resilience Model:

1. Family and Peer Support

2. Gender Role Satisfaction

3. Global and Physical Self-Esteem

4. Coping Strategies and Critical Thinking Skills

5. Holistic Wellness and Balance

These preventative factors were developed with adolescent girls in mind, yet they easily can be applied to boys and younger children as well. National Eating Disorders Association reports the clinical presentation of males is similar if not indistinguishable from eating disorders and body dysmorphia in females (Shiltz, 2005) with the exception of aspiring to family and peer pressure, media images, and societal stereotypes, which reinforce gender roles.

Smith and Niemi (2007) explored gender bias as it relates to educator perceptions of small boys in kindergarten. They submit that a boy's body size predisposes teachers to judge him as less academically capable and discuss the potential long-term consequences stating, "If a boy perceives that his teacher thinks he is unintelligent, he may conduct himself according to this perception" (p. 335). Concerned with adolescent males, Hendel (2006) states, "Self-esteem in males [tends to] increase until the age of 14. After that time, with the transition from middle school to high school, they tend to have a decline in self-esteem. . . . Most self-esteem issues in this age group are school and performance related, especially for males who do not fit the stereotypical model of what it means to be male."

CLOTHING, HAIR, AND MAKEUP

Beauty and fashion are now industries—*an activity that many people are involved in, especially one that has become commercialized or standardized.* It is also an industry that targets younger and younger consumers. Not only is this an issue of potential aesthetic bias but also one which instills conformity and pressures children and adolescents via status and economy. Girls and many boys go to great lengths to look like their media idols and peer prototypes, or to signal their social status and success through clothing, shoes, and hairstyles. Girls begin to wear makeup at younger and younger ages. Boys often associate company branding with masculinity or standing within their cultural community of peers.

Leeza was a lovely young girl with a hardworking single mom. Leeza came into counseling with several issues, but the one that lingered was anger that she didn't have "things." When I asked what "things" she needed, she said, "You know—things like other girls." Leeza wanted pretty clothes, and even though her mother was very good at fixing her hair, she wanted to have her hair done at the beauty shop. She also wanted to go to the mall with her friends and shop for "nice clothes."

At first, I thought Leeza's perseveration was a defense. I thought she was deflecting her anger about other matters onto her mother because it was safer. I worked with her in every way I knew to extract the "real" reason for her anger and increasing grief until one day she wailed, "You're not listening! I need to feel normal. I need to feel pretty, and I don't want to wear the same clothes every day! Everyone knows they come from Good Will, and I'm on the lunch program, and they call me names! They say I'm an old bag lady and that I smell bad. I just want some perfume and lip gloss and a new pair of jeans that fit me! I want Mom to get the gas bill paid so we can have heat again, and I can take a shower every day!"

I have yet to find a clinical cure for poverty.

Another quandary I have encountered repeatedly is that of girls, mothers, and hair. Almost every child or adolescent female I have counseled has had conflicts with her mother about hair. I understand this as a woman whose mother had beautiful hair that she hated and a need to fix mine in the most hideous of ways. This is, in many ways, a right of passage for women—separating our own hair from our mother's need to control it.

I have also often been privy to a curious issue between mothers and daughters of African decent. Because of my whiteness, young girls have often felt it was safe to vent to me about the issue of "good hair" and how to take care of it. Often, teens will tell me about how bad their hair is or how they wish they had good hair. Because of my professional interest in multiculturalism and my personal friendships with women of color and mothers of biracial and/or multiracial children, I know about the politicization of hair. I have not experienced the secrecy Chris Rock talks about regarding his movie *Good Hair* (Stilson, 2009) because my child clients are not often concerned (yet) with the horrible legacy of slavery and racism that impacts the biases and business of black hair. They are instead worried they are expected to know how to take care of their own hair and they don't. Repeatedly, mothers tell me their daughters are just lazy or lying. Perhaps this is also because I am white.

The movie itself has raised controversy. Rock has gotten criticism for "putting business in the street," not addressing the movement among black women to let their hair go "natural," and not pointing out that women of all races and ethnicities have issues with their hair and try to change it. Ayana Byrd, co-author of *Hair Story: Untangling Roots of Black Hair in America* (Byrd & Tharp, 2002), says, "The point is not to say hair is good or bad" but to work through the history so that "little black girls are going to be able to decide that whatever they want to do with their hair is the same as deciding what kind of earrings to put on or what dress to wear."

BODY ART AND PIERCING

Once considered a sign of societal rebellion and antiauthority, body art and piercings have become nearly mainstream in recent years. Debate persists regarding the motivations for these and other "body modifications." Carroll and Anderson (2002) cite Houghton et al. (1995) in noting that many adults obtained tattoos in late adolescence and did so due to a desire to improve appearance, perceiving tattooing as a viable art form. They further note that alternative explanations include the following:

1. Body art constitutes a statement of control or ownership over one's body and is an expression of individuality and uniqueness.

2. Body art is a means of identifying and affiliating with a group.

3. Body art is a manifestation of self-destructive impulses and may be a form of self-mutilation.

Schutz (1998) constructed an "integrated taxonomy" of self-presentational styles based upon extensive research of other authors. From these, she distinguished four styles of self-presentation: assertive, offensive, protective, and defensive. She is careful to point out, "It is not possible to ascribe a single . . . style to a particular individual, because people use different styles at different times," and they may overlap.

My own clinical experience and opinion of individuals who have tattoos and piercings—adolescents and young adults primarily—has shifted over the past few years. At one time, my clients were more inclined to have both or either out of rebellious or counter-culture attitudes and accompanying acting out behavior. It was not uncommon for these body modifications to be signals of drug use, self-harm, and/or sexual risk taking. While these issues are still present in my caseload, they have subsided. Today, these are common forms of self-expression. As an art therapist, I may have entrée into what Carroll and Anderson (2002) describe as clients' perception of "body as project" and "acts of self-creation," which are indicators of self-confidence and/or desire to record one's history as reclamation.

Conversely, Suris, Jeannin, Chossis, and Michaud (2007) cite studies which show body art and, more specifically, piercing becoming normative among adolescents, though their results indicate that piercing in particular is a marker for risk-taking behaviors and negative academic performance. They also maintain that pierced adolescents reported being less satisfied with their bodies than their unpierced counterparts, although they also state that the main reason young people obtain a piercing is a sense of uniqueness or self-expression and allow that these reasons may be a desire to increase body satisfaction.

BRACES, SCARS, AND ACNE

We often say, "Kids can be cruel," but so can adults. As a child, I received the most intrusive comments or questions about my scars from adults. I remember exasperation with children and sometimes even sadness for them because they didn't "know better," but the incidents with adults stand out most to me. Sometimes, it was out of sheer nosiness, sometimes out of ignorance, but many times those questions or comments came from a place of pity, which frankly enraged me.

We may not think of life circumstances such as braces or acne as special populations, but we do need to be conscious that the children who contend with these events or conditions feel very much outside the norm, and they are constantly reminded of that feeling by peers and siblings and sometimes even well-meaning adults. Drawing attention to braces or acne may be done in an effort to help, but the bias within this kind of helping reinforces there is something wrong with the child; something needs to be corrected, fixed, or undone.

My own childhood experience includes countless adults asking me, "Why haven't you had cosmetic surgery?" and more than once, offering to pay for it if my family couldn't. I was never sure what to say to that—because I "knew better" than to be rude—but I had many fine retorts I kept to myself. "No thank you; I'm trying to cut down" became my favorite secret response because by the time I was five, I was a veteran of reconstructive surgeries. My family had been told any further procedures would need to wait until I was fully grown. That story for another day. I cannot say that I embrace my scars, but I do live with them comfortably.

CULTURAL CONSIDERATIONS

- Watch, listen, and learn what is happening in your school. Find out who's "in" and who is "out" and what's considered "dope" these days. (ASCA National Model Standards—A.1.a., b., c., A.3.a., b., B.1.a., b., E.1.a., b., c., E.2.a., b., c., d.)

- Research the trends in popular media. (ASCA National Model Standards—B.1.d., B.2.d., C.1.c., D.2.a., b.)

- Extend the climate of inclusion to issues of aesthetics and status. (ASCA National Model Standards—A.3.b., E.1.a., b., c., E.2.a., b., c., d.)

- Be proactive in enforcement of consequences for exclusion, prejudicial talk, or behavior without creating backlash. (ASCA National Model Standards—E.1.a., b., c., E.2.a., b., c., d., F.1.a., b., d.)

- Realize that these trends may be directly or indirectly reinforced by our own or other professionals' attitudes about beauty, fashion. Respond to this in the same gentle and nonthreatening manner you would regarding other forms of bigotry or intolerance by colleagues. (ASCA National Model Standards—E.2.a., b., c., d., F.1.a., b., d., F.2.b., c., G.1., 2., 3., 4.)

- Bring in experts on body image and nutrition to present both to students and professionals. (ASCA National Model Standards—A.1.a., b., c., d., E.2.b., d., F.1.c., F.2.b.)

- Consult with administration, school nurses, dieticians, and food service professionals about expanding positive food choices and eliminating snack and soda machines. (ASCA National Model Standards—A.1.a., b., c., d., F.1.c., E.2.b., d., F.2.b.)

STRATEGIES TO SUPPORT AND FACILITATE CULTURALLY CONSIDERATE COUNSELING

- Invite your students to read, write, and share information about their peer group. Similar to strategies to elicit students' perceptions of their family heritage or history, leave the request open-ended. Do not define the topic for them and be clear they will not be graded on their acceptance of this invitation.

- Invite your students to make a peer family portrait. Invite them to tell the story behind the portrait setting.

- Invite students to create an entertainment newspaper about the "stars" of their school. Be clear they must be responsible in their reporting. They must only print facts and use reliable sources for their information.

- Ask your students the following question: *Who do you admire most in our school?* Ask them to elaborate on what they admire about that person. Be aware of how you respond to the reasons you feel are superficial versus those you feel are meaningful. Explore this further with your students.

- Remember that aesthetic issues are fraught with creative expression, longing, pride, and remorse. Be especially gentle in your approach with student clients who you may feel are shallow or narcissistic. These students may be more vulnerable or at risk than others.

CHAPTER SUMMARY

Adult clients rarely ask about my facial scars, the absence of affect, the difference in my speech. Children, age four and younger, almost always do. Adolescents will try desperately to hide their curiosity and will often shrug when I ask if they would like me to tell them.

The young children taught me the importance of telling and how to tell it in a way meaningful to them, not to me. The first time a child client asked, "What's wrong with you?" I was immediately taken back to my own grade-school experiences. Thankfully, with the help of my littlest clients, I honed my skills and tempered my response. Regardless of age, clients don't really want to know the exceptionally complex details of my medical history. They want to know very simple things. They want to know clearly and succinctly how I came to be as I am. They often want to know how old I was. They need to know that no one hurt me, and they need to know that I am okay now. Three- and four-year-olds need to know I can eat.

If small children taught me how to answer the questions, adolescent clients with eating and body image issues disorders taught me the great importance of ourselves as therapeutic mirrors. Once, many years ago, a very petite client with body distortion and a history of bulimia became quite agitated with me during an attempt to intervene in her health-threatening behaviors. She finally blurted out, "Well, if you were not overweight yourself, I might listen to you."

At the time, I was overweight. I did not feel my physical best, but I was clear about the reasons and where it fit on my self-care priority list. I waited for my countertransference to subside before I responded, "Kelly, this is about you, not me."

She was quick to snap back, "But don't you think it makes a difference? If you aren't able to control your weight, how could you help me control mine?"

"The issue isn't about weight. It is about discomfort and distortion. I am clear how my body looks, and I am comfortable with that for the time being. It is very different for you. You are underweight but feel large; you purge to control a distortion, and as a result, you are in constant discomfort."

She started to cry. "Don't you ever feel bad about yourself?"

"I wonder if what you really want to know is whether you will ever feel good about yourself." She cried harder but nodded emphatically.

"Yes, Kelly," I reassured her. "You will."

Years later, I was seeing another girl who often reminded me of Kelly. There were many differences in their external lives, but the internal worlds could have been molded from the same gritty clay. This client, Emma, was young, attractive, and slim, and always worried about her appearance, her weight, and being "right" in all that she did. Often, she would choose boyfriends who were handsome and athletic or girlfriends who were popular, perfect, and thin. If they disappointed her in some way, she could be quite cutting and crude.

During one session, she was angry at a friend for something she had done and began a litany of insults, most of which had nothing to do with the girl's actions but her physical appearance. After several grueling minutes of processing this, she was able to stop herself and admit her own self-hatred. When she did something to disappoint herself, she felt huge and ugly and imperfect. This hatred spread to her family, friends, and teachers.

I felt it would have been a therapeutic sin of omission had I not asked, "Emma, what is it like to have a therapist who is not perfect?"

She lifted her tear-stained face up, tilted her head in honest confusion. "What do you mean?"

"I mean, how is it for you that I have scars?"

"It's fine." I waited a few moments as it sunk in. "I don't know how you do it. I admire you. I could never do it. How do you cope? I mean, you seem like you cope." Then she broke down. "How *do* you cope? You seem so comfortable with yourself, and I can't even go out of the house if I have a pimple. Some days, I'm even jealous of you. Isn't that weird?"

Although my countertransference was present, I was actually saddened for her, exhausted by the endless search for fantasy. "Emma, there is no such thing as perfect. It has always been like this for me. When you know from the beginning that perfection can never be, it is much easier to accept who you already are in the moment."

This, I believe, is our challenge as helping professionals. There can be no perfect, but there can be comfort and self-acceptance. We can impart this to our child clients through unconditional positive regard, and we can provide models and mirrors through our own self-awareness and comfort. To do otherwise is disingenuous. Children and teens have extraordinary radar and will spot chinks in our armor a mile away. They instinctively recognize if we are unable to see ourselves without bias, we will be unable to see them.

5

Illness

SEVERE AND CHRONIC MEDICAL CONDITIONS

Nabors and Lehmkuhl (2004) utilize Stein and colleagues' definition of chronic conditions as those lasting more than one year and produce

> . . . limitations of function, activities, or social role in comparison with healthy age peers in the general areas of physical, cognitive, emotional, or social development. In addition, these conditions may cause dependency and requirements for special care for youth in one or more areas such as . . . medications, special diet, medical technology, assistive devices, and personal assistance.

Although the list is endless and varied in severity, some of the more common chronic conditions include asthma, diabetes, gastrointestinal disorders, and various cancers. While learning about the illness or condition of a specific student is helpful to the individual child, understanding the issues common to many children with chronic medical conditions provides a well-rounded background for working with any student and his or her family (Nabors & Lehmkuhl, 2004).

The Surgeon General outlined a "family centered" model of care in 1987, emphasizing family needs and strengths, impact of cultural influence, and development level of children with chronic medical conditions. Malchiodi (1999) gives three primary sources of stress in pediatric patients:

1. Separation from parents or caretakers through hospitalization

2. Loss of independence and control

3. Fears and anxieties about medical procedures that may cause harm or fear and fear of death (p. 11)

She also notes that age and developmental factors contribute to how a child is affected. Infants, toddlers, and preschoolers will be most vulnerable to separation. Children between five to eight years will be more fearful of procedures and pain, while older children may become more concerned about death and the meaning of death.

Nabors and Lehmkuhl (2004) cite Rynard in itemizing the key roles for school mental health professionals:

1. Helping children cope with frequent absences

2. Providing counseling and support for parents and children

3. Teaching children strategies for medical fears

4. Assisting children and families who must manage side effects related to medical care

5. Developing interventions for the classroom as well as emergency medical plans

6. Consulting and collaborating with parents, school staff, and medical team

7. Assisting in developing educational plans and developing plans to improve adherence to medication regimes, self-care at school, or classroom behaviors

8. Assessing and intervening to improve academic and cognitive functioning

9. Providing counseling and guidance for children to facilitate their coping with emotional and behavioral problems

Developing school reentry programs are also important to the reintegration of a child into the classroom and school system. Providing information to school staff and teachers, administration, and school nurses prior to a child returning to school can be very beneficial to the identified student and also for schoolwide comfort. Specific goals of reentry programs include (1) sustaining or improving attendance and academic achievement, (2) educating classmates about the child's condition to facilitate understanding and foster peer relationships, (3) teacher education and support, and (4) family support (Nabors & Lehmkuhl, 2004, p. 6). Family support includes siblings, and school counselors may find they need to address the secondary stress of other children in the family.

Nabors and Lehmkuhl (2004) note that about 40% of children with chronic medical conditions do experience some type of school-related problem. Support centering on coping strategies, psychosocial, and educational issues benefits school functioning and peer acceptance. Children with chronic medical conditions may report feeling "different" from peers for many reasons. They may return to school with physical challenges, or they may look different, which can lead to peer rejection or self-isolation. Similarly, children with central nervous system impairments resulting from the condition or treatment and/or children who are cognitively challenged are at greater risk of poor social acceptance and adjustment problems.

Medications may impact a child's academic ability or ability to relate to classmates because of mood alterations or lethargy. Anxiety and depression are also common as a result of repeated treatment or hospitalization. Anticipatory anxiety and fear are not uncommon if a child is continuing to receive treatment or needs repetitive hospitalizations. In some instances, obsessive-compulsive symptoms emerge. Studies have also shown a propensity for post-traumatic stress and/or dissociative disorders following intensive hospitalizations and invasive medical procedures (Coskun & Zoroglu, 2009).

It took many years for me to understand that I am a survivor of medical trauma. I had been treating survivors of trauma for many years and knew I had a great understanding of and empathy for their symptomology, but I did not recognize this as countertransferential for many years, primarily because it did not interfere with my work; rather, my work was informed by it.

In graduate school, I began therapy for very typical reasons: academic anxiety, family disruption, my first "real" relationship. I really didn't like therapy much (clinicians are almost always thorny clients), but I persevered. My therapist was a "gentle prodder." She taught me much about myself and much about how to be a therapist. The thing for which I am most grateful, both as client and clinician, was her ability to truly attend and weed my gnarly internal garden. It would have been easy for both of us to decide I must have been sexually abused, but I was not. I readily claimed every other family dysfunction but could not claim that one because it wasn't mine. Susanna helped me reclaim the validity of my medical trauma, to understand it was enough, and I had a right to my anxieties, body memories, and hatred of seat belts and being cold.

In turn, I became far more discerning in my own practice, being attuned to client history, life events, and secondary situations, which might produce symptoms and reactions more easily attributable to other circumstances. Chelsea taught me the importance of truly *listening* and *seeing* what a child knows about herself.

Chelsea was referred to me for adjunct art therapy by another child therapist who felt "stuck." Chelsea was eight years old, bright, but having some problems academically. She was unfocused and often found "daydreaming" in class. When it came time to go to gym, she would often go to the nurse's office because she felt sick at her stomach. She was failing science, but her scores in other classes remained high.

The therapist who referred Chelsea reported some increased difficulty at home. Chelsea had begun to become agitated and disrespectful, especially around bath and bedtime. Chelsea finally did admit sleep disturbance, and her mother had discovered recently she was wetting the bed but getting up in the middle of the night and washing the bedclothes herself so no one would find out. The referring therapist was convinced Chelsea had been sexually abused and on the surface, her symptomology fit; however, Chelsea denied anyone ever touching her inappropriately, and her mother was extremely upset by the thought.

Chelsea was referred to me because I specialized in treating sexual trauma victims and survivors but also because of my art therapy credentials. The referring therapist wanted to continue to see Chelsea but wanted a second opinion. She also hoped art therapy might be able to tell us something Chelsea could not say in words.

I began by interviewing Chelsea and her mother. Both told me essentially the same things they had told the other therapist. When I gently broached the subject of sexual abuse, her mother began to cry. Chelsea rolled her eyes. "I keep telling them nothing happened to me like that." I believed her; there was no hesitancy in her voice, and her frustration with the adults trying to help her was clear. I asked if she knew what was going on with her grades and nightmares, but she only shrugged and shook her head.

The plan was for me to see Chelsea a total of three to six times and to use art as an assessment tool and perhaps as an interventive method. In the first sessions, I invited Chelsea to engage in creating assessment images: House-Tree-Person, Draw a Person Doing Something, and a Kinetic Family Drawing. These pictures indicated agitation and self-protection, but as child therapeutic artwork goes, they were relatively unremarkable. During the fourth session, I invited Chelsea to create a free drawing or image. She created a portrait of a female sitting down with many people around her standing up. The female was childlike and wide-eyed. The standing figures seemed to be adults and were virtually all the same. I asked her to tell me about the picture.

"I don't know. It's just a picture."

"Is this a person you know?" I asked, pointing to the girl in the chair. Chelsea shook her head. "How about these people? Who are they?"

"They're the Cold People," she said.

"Tell me about the Cold People."

"Their hands are cold, and they make you cold," Chelsea said quietly.

"How do you know about the Cold People?"

"I dream about them. I don't like to dream about them. I have to get up."

"Is that when you have the pee accidents in your bed?" I asked using the term she had previously used to describe the bedwetting.

She nodded.

"How old is the girl in the chair?" I asked.

"I don't know. Maybe two." The figure looked closer to Chelsea's current age, but I did not comment. I also noticed two tiny dots on both legs of the child figure. I asked Chelsea to tell me about those.

She frowned. "I don't know. But I have some, too." Chelsea then pulled up her pant legs and showed me two small circular scars on the side of each leg.

"Do you know where those dots came from?"

Chelsea shook her head. "I've always had 'em. Mom calls them my angel kisses."

"Do you know why she calls them that?"

"Not really," Chelsea said. "She just says that the angels came and made my legs better one day and they left kisses."

Chelsea's mother helped to shed light on the mystery. When Chelsea was a toddler, she had been in a car accident that broke both of her legs and killed her father. Chelsea knew about the accident that took her father but did not remember being hospitalized. She had to have surgery to correct the breakage, was routinely catheterized, and wore casts for several months, but in her mother's mind, it was relatively minor compared to the loss of her husband. Chelsea never asked, and her mother never explained other than to tell her the story of the "angel kisses" when she was about four years old.

Further sessions with Chelsea clarified what contributed to the onset of Chelsea's current problems. Mom was dating for the first time since her husband had died; Chelsea had been asked about the scars on her knees by another little girl when she was changing clothes for gym; and in science class, the sinks were like those in a hospital. Chelsea was reexperiencing physiological and emotional reactions to the events surrounding her father's death and her hospitalization, but she had no clear cognitive memory with which to connect them. As we worked with images, she was able to begin to integrate the details her mother shared with her with the pictures that spontaneously came out onto paper. She eventually stopped coming to see me and returned to her original therapist to continue cognitive behavioral therapy to improve her functioning at school and home.

EMOTIONAL AND MENTAL HEALTH CONCERNS

Realizing my population base is somewhat skewed, it is still difficult for me to ascertain why so many children and adolescents today carry mental health diagnoses. I wonder about the prevalence of dysfunctional or abusive homes, drugs and alcohol, a society inundated by graphic violence, media manipulation, and video games. I wonder if this war is different than other wars. I wonder if global warming or pesticides have done something to our drinking water. I understand the dismissal of flawed studies connecting vaccines to autism, yet I cannot easily dismiss the anecdotal evidence of thousands of parents nor the influence of pharmaceutical corporations. I wonder if for each child taking amphetamines for hyperactivity there is really an adult who should be taking lorazepam for anxiety.

I wonder these things, yet I also have witnessed the pain of children who were not in control of the thoughts in their heads or the behaviors they displayed. I have seen the relief brought about by the right combination of therapy and medication.

More common mental health issues seen in schools are mood, anxiety, adjustment, and attachment disorders. These students may also be identified as having "severe emotional disturbance" and qualify for special education services under the Individuals with Disabilities Education Act (IDEA) (2004). If special education services are needed, and the child is eligible under the IDEA, the school district must develop an Individualized Education Program that addresses his or her specific needs.

Though it is not commonly seen in the classroom, children can be diagnosed with psychotic disorders, which include symptoms of paranoia, delusions, and hallucinations. Optimistically, by the time a child reaches school age, he or she has been diagnosed and is in treatment. While the student is still entitled to "free appropriate public education," regardless of the nature or severity of his or her disability per Section 504 of the Rehabilitation Act of 1973, alternative schooling or residential care may be better for a child with severe and chronic psychosis.

For children with mental illness, change can be difficult. Providing a predictable routine and stabile school environment is very helpful. As with any illness, limitation, or difference, allow the child to tell about his condition in his own way, in his own time. Diagnoses will mean little to many teachers and nothing to other students. Understanding the struggles a child faces or the compensations she must make to be successful in school is far more important than a label.

CULTURAL CONSIDERATIONS

- Learn about medical conditions and mental illness but don't get caught up in the details of complicated diagnoses. Remember the student has specialists to attend to these needs. (ASCA National Model Standards—E.2.a., b., c., d., D.1.g.)

- Concentrate on strengths. Support wellness. Never use words such as "terminal" or "untreatable." (ASCA National Model Standards—B.2.a., b., c., d., E.2.a., b., c., d.)

- Ask students to teach you and their peers about both their challenges and triumphs. (ASCA National Model Standards—A.1.a., b., c., B.1.d., E.2.)

- Be willing to talk about your own obvious illnesses in a direct, yet boundaried way. (ASCA National Model Standards—E.1.a., b., E.2.c.)

- Be sensitive to students if they are not yet willing or able to discuss their illnesses with peers or others. Let them know you have information from other sources in order to help them best at school. (ASCA National Model Standards—A.1.a., b., c., d., E.2.a.)

- Expect as much from students with illnesses as you do from others but make sure they have access and resources to assist in achievement academically, emotionally, and creatively. (ASCA National Model Standards—A.1.a., b., c., d., B.1.d., D.1.g., E.2.a.)

- Be an advocate for schoolwide acceptance. (ASCA National Model Standards—A.1.a., b., c., d., B.1.d., D.1.g., E.2.a.)

STRATEGIES TO SUPPORT AND FACILITATE CULTURALLY CONSIDERATE COUNSELING

- Examine your thoughts, feelings, beliefs, and experiences regarding illness. Do you feel medical conditions are more legitimate than mental illness?

- Invite your students to describe how their illness affects an average day at school. Ask how you can help to make school easier and sustain the things that already do.

- Invite all students to keep a wellness journal using written and visual entries. Not only can this be a good source of release for your students, but it can also be a good way to monitor the wellbeing of children with illness without separating them from their peers.

- Visit hospital wards and residential facilities. Become familiar with what a child experiences in the hospital or inpatient settings.

- Encourage your school to adopt Universal Design for Learning.

- Work with school food services to ensure dietary needs of students with medical conditions are met. Also, remember that some psychotropic medication will interact negatively with some foods and make sure students are protected.

- Write a health history of your own. Consider how your own history of medical or mental health treatment may impact how you view your students.

CHAPTER SUMMARY

Children who are (or have been) seriously or chronically ill, have been hospitalized, or have undergone medical treatment have specific psychosocial needs. Reactions and needs vary from child to child, but there are some experiences common to most pediatric patients. Emotional distress is frequent during and after illness and/or hospitalization. Factors such as the initial environment in which the child is seen may affect his or her response. The nature of the specific condition or illness (acute, chronic, or circumstantial) impacts the child's reaction. Most critical to the child's adjustment is the quality of familial and/or caregiver support before, during, and after treatment or hospitalization (Malchiodi, 1999).

School counselors, teachers, and adjunct personnel can assist in a child's recovery and reentry by providing safe and consistent support during the school day and keeping in contact with parents and other caregivers regarding the student client's ongoing health and mental health related needs.

6

Environmental Issues

A dults may bring their work home with them; children often bring their home lives to school. As educators and professional helpers, we have an obligation to be sensitive to how circumstances outside the classroom affect performance within class.

ABUSE AND VIOLENCE AT HOME

Domestic violence between parents and physical, sexual, emotional, and psychological violence take an enormous toll on families and certainly on children. There is a dearth of information and resources about child abuse and neglect, child sexual trauma, and the aftereffects of domestic violence upon children. For many years, I specialized in treating adults and children who were victims/survivors of abuse and violence as well as training other professionals to do the same. It is intricate work, which must be individualized to the client, the history, and the supportive systems in place during the therapy/healing process. While I am a believer that no child can ever have enough caring adults in his or her life, I do caution that treatment should be done outside of school and beyond the scope of most school counselors' job descriptions or time constraints. There are other important contributions to a child's healing, which can be made within a school setting.

School counselors and educators should be made aware of a student's history and involvement in current treatment if they are not already. Ideally, contact between school professionals and the primary therapist should be maintained. This of course involves releases signed by adult caregivers and should also be agreeable to the student client. Purposes of the contact are best limited to school performance, behavior, and symptomology which might be seen at school. School professionals can help by sharing academic changes, emotional outbursts, and peer interactions with the therapist. Primary therapists can help by suggesting ways in which the student might be assisted while at school and in some instances, reasons for changes in achievement, behavior, or absenteeism.

Becoming familiar with symptoms of adjustment disorder, post-traumatic stress, dissociation, and anxiety disorders can be useful. If the child also has special needs, recognizing the extended challenges of abuse and violence for these children can be extremely helpful.

In the context of helping without bias, here are some things to keep in mind:

- The nature of abuse and/or violence puts all children in a position to feel as if they are different, less than, alien.
- Safety is of utmost importance, but what makes a child feel safe may shift and change.
- Legalities may be complicated; it is imperative to find out who has custody of the child and have documents on file. All personnel should be made aware if there are any restrictions in who has access to the child.
- Maintaining boundaries is extremely important; an abused child may have few (or no exposure to) appropriate boundaries, and it is the job of safe adults to reflect proper ones.
- Many helping professionals and many educators have histories of abuse or other types of violence as children and adolescents. It is important to recognize when a student's situation is triggering feelings or memories and to consult a supervisor or therapist if these become intrusive in daily functioning or work with a particular child.

HARASSMENT, BULLYING, AND SCHOOL VIOLENCE

Gossip and rumor may be a part of the average school experience; children and adolescents in today's society often contend with a new level of intrusion and a greater sense of harm. My experience and instinct tells me the world we live in today is more violent and crude, and fosters an unprecedented level of entitlement. We are exposed to dysfunctional drama daily through reality shows and entertainment news. Social networking has made us feel guilty if we don't respond to someone's invitation to Facebook or MySpace, as if we are the offending party. Bloggers and tweets give us up-to-the-minute and minute-by-minute minutia about one another and about complete strangers. Mobile phones give us 24-hour access, and call waiting has made not answering the phone a communal crime.

Of all these dynamics, I believe this collective sense of entitlement is the most dangerous and potentially damaging for our young people. I also believe it is a major factor in the increase of harassment and bullying in schools. Taken to the extreme, it may be a factor in school violence.

Verbal harassment, rumor spreading, gossip, insufferable teasing or insults, and social exclusion increase with age, peaking in early adolescence. Consequences may be extremely detrimental in that the impact extends beyond individuals and involves peer groups, compromising a child's entire social peer group and other members of the group as well. Research has shown that perception of risk can create fear for one's personal safety, even without personal experience of risk or danger (Cross & Peisner, 2009).

Cross and Peisner (2009) suggest a unique prevention approach that addresses the concerns of rumor spreading and uses the very vehicle which may contribute to the problem in the first place. By instituting a "social norms" campaign, the approach promotes healthy behaviors through identifying problem behaviors, then using a variety of media to advertise the true behavioral norm for the behavior among the specific population of students. Billboards, television ads, radio announcements, t-shirts, and screen-savers are among some of the ways in which social norms can be communicated. Cross and Peisner note that in their sample, students spread rumors because they thought other kids were doing it, not because they viewed rumor spreading positively.

Children and adolescents who are victims of harassment or bullying are often anxious, insecure, cautious, and have low self-esteem. They rarely defend themselves when confronted and are often socially isolated and lack age-appropriate social skills. When bullied, children feel tense, anxious, and afraid. Effects of bullying may be lack of concentration, withdrawal, depression, regression, and avoidance of school or school activities.

Parents and educators instinctively protect children from being bullied, harassed, or treated badly by their peers. A less natural and more difficult task is how to deal with a child who is the instigator of aggression toward others. Recently, much has been written about the dynamics of bullying and interventions after the fact, but little attention has been given to how to address the bullying behavior of our own children. While some children do engage in bullying behavior because they fear being brunt of jokes, ridicule, and physical abuse by peers, research actually suggests bullies often feel superior to others, have high self-esteem, do well in school, and are popular with classmates and teachers.

As parents and educators, we hope these things work themselves out on their own, but in real time, they rarely do. The word itself—"bully"—may diminish the seriousness of the problem. Television show characters

Eddie Haskell and Nellie Oleson were bullies. My clients BJ, Tiffany, and Brian were violent boys and girls. BJ broke his grandmother's wrist trying to wrangle the remote control from her. Tiffany sent a classmate to the hospital after a fight on the playground because the other girl was looking at her funny. Brian set fire to the school science lab trying to show his friends how to "cook up meth." Bullying is about intimidation and violence and will only be stopped when knowledgeable adults are willing to confront the children they love about behaviors of hate.

Characteristics of children and adolescents who bully may seem generally positive. Self-confidence, high self-esteem, physical aptitudes, and leadership qualities are not predictors of bullying but are useful traits for exerting dominance. Add impulsivity, quick temper, low tolerance for frustration, and enthusiasm for violent games, movies, and other activities and the likelihood of bullying increases. A child or teen exhibiting these characteristics and who exhibits little or no empathy for others is at great risk for bullying behavior.

Warning signs may include the following:

- Taunting, extreme name-calling, and physical harm of siblings
- Cruelty toward animals
- Obsession with violent media such as games, music, or movies
- Recurrent bruising or contusions on hands, arms, and face
- Lack of an emotional vocabulary
- Grandiosity
- Disrespectful attitudes toward peers
- Verbalization of aggressive fantasies
- Bragging about unkind or hurtful behaviors toward others
- Lack of respect for authority

Adults need to realize that bullying may be physical but may also be verbal, psychological, or emotional. Name-calling, rumors, shaming, social isolation, and sexual harassment are in many cases just as damaging as bodily harm. Bullying is serious. It is not about pranks or teasing. It is dangerous and often a precursor to antisocial or criminal behaviors. Bullying happens in every school environment regardless of community, geography, socioeconomic condition, or demographic makeup. Bullying takes place on the school bus, on the playground, in the cafeteria, in bathrooms, in cyberspace, in hallways, and even in the classroom with the teacher present. Bullying behavior is perpetrated by both boys and girls. Although there is indication that boys are more prone to physical aggression, incidents of physical injury by girls are increasing.

Bullying is *not* about conflict. There is nothing to "work out" between the victim and victimizer. Bullying is an aggressive behavior inflicted on one person by another for no reason other than a perceived power differential. Conflict resolution and mediation may send inadvertent messages that there is equal responsibility between the children involved or, worse, may further victimize a child who has been the target of bullying. Kids who are bullied do not need to "toughen up." It is the bully who must change his or her behavior, and adults must make sure the change takes place.

Recognition of school-based aggression has increased over the past decade. While it is difficult to determine whether this is because bullying has increased, the following factors are considered:

- Prevalence of graphic media violence and ease of access to cable television, Internet, and other electronic devices
- Reality television and shock jock radio
- Decrease in consistent adult supervision as a result of single-parent, dual-income households and staggered work schedules stemming from economic hardship and war
- Elimination of many afterschool programs because of budget cuts or redistribution
- Increase in child and adolescent psychosocial diagnoses, such as attention deficit/hyperactivity disorders, pervasive development disorders, and conduct disorders

Regardless of cause, parents and schools must work together to address bullying.

Obviously, school violence poses even greater problems for school communities, but it must be noted that in many instances of school-based violence, bullying was one of many mediating factors. In instances where there was a single victim, interpersonal disputes were the primary motive.

A trend for multiple victim events has increased since the early 1990s. An event in an Arizona middle school is cited as the first such event, and the Columbine High School attack in Colorado, resulting in 13 homicides and two suicides, has been the largest of such events to date (Logue, 2008).

A 2008 article in *Professional School Counseling* discussed four lessons for school counselors responding to serious crisis such as school shootings:

1. School counselors can expect to take on leadership roles in times of crisis due to their expertise.

2. Crisis teams are temporary organizations within a school structure and may create role conflict.

3. Effective school counselors have found subtle ways to support and counsel formal leaders.

4. School counselors must be vigilant in their own care during a school crisis. (Fein, Carlisle, & Isaacson, 2008)

Terminology such as "lockdown drills," "search and rescue," and "triage sites" were not in school policy manuals just a few short years ago. The demand for trained crisis leadership has forced new roles for all school personnel, particularly administrators and school counselors (Fein, Carlisle, & Isaacson, 2008).

DISASTERS

Donna Gaffney (2006) writes,

> There are a number of events that can thrust children into frac-
> tured versions of their former lives, including the death of a par-
> ent, divorce, illness, and the usual assortment of life transitions.
> As clinicians, we begin repair work, assessing the nature of the
> crisis and the child's response, identifying needs and resources to
> assist the family as they begin to resolve the situation. . . . Trauma
> and traumatic loss are pervasive clinical phenomena confronting
> children and their families. Although the goals of immediate and
> long-term interventions are to alleviate distress, restore pre-crisis
> functioning, and integrate the traumatic event into a child's life,
> some children will always view the trauma as the signature event
> of their existence. It becomes the marker separating their pre-event
> and post-event selves. (pp. 1001–1002)

The events of September 11, hurricanes Katrina and Rita, tsunamis,
and now earthquakes in Haiti and Chile and the Gulf oil disaster surpass
the word "trauma" in the enormity of the events and the resulting consequences to total societies. Children of these disasters were forced to face
death, destruction of home and community, forced upheaval, and insta-
bility caused by family separations. In addition, adults who ordinarily
would be protectors and healers were equally devastated.

CULTURAL CONSIDERATIONS

- Listen carefully; ask questions; do not assume. (ASCA National
  Model Standards—A.1.a., b., c., 3.a., b., B.1.a, b., E.1.a., b., c., E.2.a.,
  b., c., d.)

- Research what your students share with you and ask them more
  questions. (ASCA National Model Standards—B.1.d., B.2.d., C.1.c.,
  D.2.a., b.)

- Construct a consistent climate of inclusion and interest within the
  school community. (ASCA National Model Standards—A.3.b., E.1.a.,
  b., c., E.2.a., b., c., d.)

- Be proactive in enforcement of consequences for exclusion, prejudicial
  talk, or behavior without creating backlash. (ASCA National Model
  Standards—E.1.a., b., c., E.2.a., b., c., d., F.1.a., b., d.)

- Learn more about post-traumatic stress. (ASCA National Model
  Standards—C.2. c., d., E.1.b., c., F.1.c.)

- Respond directly and swiftly to incidents of bullying or violence in your school. (ASCA National Model Standards—A.7.a., b., C.2.b., D.1.a., b., D.2.a., b., c., f., g.)
- Take a class on emergency medical assistance or crisis management. (ASCA National Model Standards—E.1.a., b., c., E.2.a., b., c., d., F.1.a., b., d.)
- Learn about the culture of students who may come to your school after being displaced by disasters. (ASCA National Model Standards—A.3.b., E.1.a., b., c., E.2.a., b., c., d.)
- Learn about the nature of the specific disaster they may have endured. (ASCA National Model Standards—B.1.d., B.2.d., C.1.c., D.2.a., b.)
- Seek other professionals who may have more personal or professional experience with a particular population. (ASCA National Model Standards—C. 1.c., d., D.1.c., E.1.c., E.2.d., F.2.a., G.1.)
- Attend professional workshops, presentations, and conferences to expand cultural and awareness and competency. (ASCA National Model Standards—E.1.c., E.2.d., G.1., 2., 3., 4.)
- Continue to listen, ask questions, and share what you've learned from your students about heritage, geography, circumstance, and relationships. (ASCA National Model Standards—A.1.a., b., c., d., F.1.c., E.2.b., d., F.2.b.)

STRATEGIES TO SUPPORT AND FACILITATE CULTURALLY CONSIDERATE COUNSELING

- Initiate conversations about bullying rather than waiting for a specific incident to arise.
- Be clear in your disapproval of aggression both in words and actions without being judgmental.
- Discuss adults who demonstrate bullying or violent behavior. Invite your students to give examples of how the situations could be handled better.
- Help children build an emotional vocabulary. Ask children to express themselves in feeling words. Encourage words beyond "fine" and "okay." Ask them to elaborate on slang words such as "dope" or "tight."
- Introduce children to a variety of types of people and situations.
- Build empathy by exposing students to people and causes in need. Demonstrate how to serve without shaming.

- Pay attention to negative or objectifying language and insist on explanations. Discuss alternative ways to speak about individuals who are different from or disliked by your child client.

- Advocate a strong zero tolerance school policy on bullying.

- Take immediate action when an incident of bullying is brought to your attention.

- Make sure to present a united adult team consisting of teachers, parents, and administrators.

- Follow through with consequences.

- Insist that children verbally acknowledge what they have done and make sincere apologies and amends to those they have hurt. Model how this may be done.

- Step up supervision and consequences if bullying behavior recurs.

- Refer for professional help if the behavior persists.

CHAPTER SUMMARY

Many things have been gleaned from the callous behavior and horrific events described in this chapter: the need for a common language among survivors and helpers, including a compassion-building vocabulary, the impact of media deluge, need for attendance to wounded helpers so they can continue to help others, the recognition of resilience. Children and adults alike exhibit coping skills that exceed anything professionals could have expected.

We have also learned things about post-traumatic stress. Researchers have identified three factors that increase children's vulnerability to post-traumatic stress disorder: physical proximity to the traumatic event, severity of the traumatic event, and reactions of primary caregivers. Factors that can further complicate a child's healing process are such things as previous trauma, inadequate social supports, and/or witnessing a death (Gaffney, 2006). Age and developmental level of the child is always a factor in treatment approaches and stabilizing process. With that in mind, Gaffney (2006) identifies the following as important to any child healing in the aftermath of disaster: trust, sanctuary, grounding, self-care, and comfort.

7

Gender and Sexuality Issues

My first feminist act was a bet I made with my father that Billie Jean King would win the infamous tennis match against Bobby Riggs. I got the dollar; Dad never quite got over it. For years, I truly thought he was joking when he would make sexist remarks. I couldn't believe my supportive, intelligent father could be that dumb. Many years later, I discovered he was actually an inflexible chauvinist and an enthusiastic Rush Limbaugh fan. By then, at least, it sent me into peals of laughter instead of back into therapy.

My focus on women's issues expanded in college. My senior project was a photojournalism essay titled "Working Women of the Ozarks." I was a research assistant in graduate school for a professor whose expertise was in older women's issues. My first clinical internship was with an agency providing services to battered women and rape survivors. While there, I participated in a program which took us into the women's state prison where we advocated for battered women who were incarcerated for killing violent partners in self-defense. I worked for the agency after graduate school and eventually opened a private practice with two other therapists who specialized in women's therapy issues.

In my original outlines, early drafts, and even this final document, I left out issues of gender equity as a cultural consideration. I spent many years of my life working on behalf of women's rights and specializing in women's therapy issues; perhaps I was hoping we had come far enough to warrant concentration elsewhere. This is a bit like saying we are in a "post-racial" America. Neither is remotely true. They are, in fact, inextricably linked.

We are still raising our daughters to be paid less than our sons. President Obama signed the Lilly Ledbetter Fair Pay Act, which sent a long overdue message, but women are still paid 78 cents for every dollar made by a man. In schools, girls are still discouraged from math and sciences. And each year, more and more boys are held back from kindergarten and first grade because they are "too immature" to begin school.

REVISITING TITLE IX

It has been nearly four decades since Congress passed Title IX, protecting educational rights for all students regardless of gender. A reminder of the equal rights enumerated by this law follows:

- The right to enroll in any course or program
- The right to be treated equitably in terms of course requirements and meeting those requirements
- The right to learn about the contributions of *all* people to the field of study
- The right to hear language that is nonsexist and non-gender biased
- The right to participate fully in all classroom discussions
- The right to be disciplined according to the nature of an offense rather than on the basis of gender
- The right to receive praise for accomplishments and constructive criticism for improving academic achievement
- The right to pursue education free of sexual harassment from other students or faculty
- The right to be considered for any work-study program or co-op job
- The right to know one's rights

Title IX requires schools to inform students of their rights and how to protect them. Each district should have a Title IX coordinator who is responsible for making sure students, teachers, school counselors, and adjunct personnel know their rights and responsibility under this law. Some schools have student advocates.

ENGENDERING EQUITY

Decades have passed since the seminal work of Carol Gilligan (*In a Different Voice,* 1993) and Mary Pipher (*Reviving Ophelia,* 1995), both of which helped us to understand the overt and covert silencing of girls, especially at adolescence, yet inequities continue today. While some say feminists pitted girls against boys, further examination reveals that boys and girls are on the same side in the struggle for equitable acceptance. Challenging sex-role stereotypes, decreasing tolerance for school violence and bullying, and increasing attention to violence at home actually enables both girls and boys to feel safer at school (Kimmel, 2000). Flood and Shaffer (2000) recall that early feminist work with girls and young women taught a great deal about the value and power of adult role models, writing that intervention is most effective when students and adults are given safe opportunities to examine gender roles openly and discuss their relationship to behavior.

Amanda Chapman (2010) writes, "There is some evidence that girls are becoming more academically successful than boys; however, examination of the classroom shows that girls and boys continue to be socialized in ways that work against gender equity." Over the past 30 years, the increased involvement of girls in athletics has correlated with both higher levels of self-esteem and reduction in dropout rates and teen pregnancy.

The current debate about school violence has largely ignored any consideration of gender as a factor. Craig Flood of the Gender and Diversities Institute and Susan Shaffer of the Mid-Atlantic Equity Center advocate intervention efforts which make aware the relationship between violence and the construction of masculinity in our culture and in our schools. According to Flood and Shaffer (2000), boys are still encouraged to "purge themselves of any softness." They write,

> The challenge for gender equity advocates is to find ways for educators to deflate the traditional concepts of masculinity that underlie violent and antisocial behaviors, and thus to limit their influence on boys' emotional development. Once they understand the links between masculinity and such behaviors, educators can identify early warning signs, search for explanations, work with schools to respond more quickly to danger signals, and develop strategies for addressing the causes. . . . (p. 3)

In describing what boys need, Kindlon and Thompson (1999) are actually describing what all children need. Adolescent boys want to "be loved, have sex, and not be hurt." They suggest adults use the following guidelines for boys: Allow them to indulge their emotions, accept a high level of physical activity, speak their language, and treat them with respect; teach that empathy is courage; use discipline to guide and build; model manhood as emotionally attached; and teach the many ways in which a boy can be a man.

Kindlon and Thompson (1999) advocate what feminists have been advocating for girls and describe "emotional illiteracy" of boys that develops from being boxed into a narrow definition of maleness by family, school, and society. This illiteracy includes a lack of emotional connection often mixed with a sense of privilege, power, and entitlement and leads to disrespectful and antisocial behaviors. Emotional intelligence is reflected through empathy and healthy interpersonal relationships. By learning empathy, boys become more understanding of others and more aware of the impact their behavior has on others (Flood & Shaffer, 2000).

Research on boys or girls would not be complete without an analysis of differences by race/ethnicity, class, and other variables. Thorne (2001) asserts we must develop further collaborative enterprises among scholars who investigate each and all dimensions of social equity in schooling. Phillips (2001) cautions us to recognize there are at least as many differences among boys and girls as there are between them, stating, "We need a better understanding of how young people experience schooling not only as boys and girls but as boys and girls from diverse backgrounds."

In adolescence, both boys and girls get their first real dose of gender inequality. Girls suppress ambition; boys inflate it. Research on academic achievement validates that girls are more likely to undervalue their abilities, especially in traditionally male-dominated subjects of math and science with only the most secure and gifted girls taking these courses, while boys often overvalue their abilities and remain in programs in which they are less qualified and able to succeed. Conversely, girls tend to succeed in English and foreign languages, but boys often disregard these subjects as "lame" or "for faggots" (Kimmel, 2000).

Boys of all ages are keenly aware of the boundaries of the masculine ideal. Emotions or feelings are considered to be "feminine" and often confused and conceptualized through homophobia (Flood & Shaffer, 2000). Michael Thompson (1999), co-author of *Raising Cain*, describes homophobia as a universal experience for males and as a "force stronger than gravity in the lives of adolescent boys" (p. 82).

In *Beyond the "Gender Wars": A Conversation About Girls, Boys, and Education*, William Pollack (2001) states, "We already know . . . that the most safe schools are those in which boys and girls can interact positively together, respect one another, and talk to each other." Campbell (2001) concurs and adds, "One of the basic things you can do in a school to make it work for both girls and boys is to instill a clear rule of no disrespect. The students are not allowed to disrespect each other; they are not allowed to disrespect teachers, nor are teachers allowed to disrespect students."

LGBTQ STUDENTS, PARENTS, AND EDUCATORS

Recently, Chastity Bono publically asked to be known as Chaz Bono. After 40 years of living as a woman, Chaz has decided to transition, eventually reconciling his internal gender with external gender characteristics. Even my first response was a wistful sigh, remembering Sonny and Cher's cute little girl in petticoats and patent leather shoes. Helping without bias does not mean we don't sometimes wish for things to be different or less complicated.

The ASCA (American School Counselor Association, 2005) position on lesbian, gay, bisexual, transgender, and questioning (LGBTQ) youth states,

> Professional school counselors promote equal opportunity and respect for all individuals regardless of sexual orientation/gender identity. Professional school counselors work to eliminate barriers that impede student development and achievement and are committed to academic, personal, social, and career development of all students.
>
> The professional school counselor works with all students through all stages of identity development and understands this development may be more difficult for LGBTQ youth. It is not the role of the professional school counselor to attempt to change a student's sexual orientation/gender identity but instead to provide support to LGBTQ students to promote student achievement and personal well-being. (American School Counselor Association, 2007)

The National Association of School Psychologists (NASP) and the American Psychological Association (APA) have similar statements. NASP adds that schools have a legal, ethical, and moral obligation to provide equal access to education and equal protection under the law for all students, noting that survival, not education, is the priority for many sexual minority students (Weller, 2003). The APA (1998) gives explicit guidelines for psychologists, the first of which is, "homosexuality and bisexuality are not indicative of mental illness." In 1973, the American Psychiatric Association removed "homosexuality" from the *Diagnostic and Statistical Manual* recognizing sexual orientation/preference is not a disorder needing to be "cured."

I have counseled many adolescents and adults who question or identify as belonging to a sexual minority. During my three decades of practice, the terms have expanded from "gay" and "lesbian" to an acronym which continues to adapt to the times and the research. Below are the acronymic terms as I currently know them, supported by definitions from LAMBDA (2009) and the National Center for Lesbian Rights (2003):

> Lesbian: An adult or adolescent female whose emotional, romantic, and sexual attractions are primarily for other women.

> Gay: A person whose emotional, romantic, and sexual attractions are primarily for individuals of the same sex, typically in reference to men.

> Bisexual: A person who is emotionally, romantically, and sexually attracted to both men and women.

Transgender: An umbrella term used to describe people whose gender expression is nonconforming and/or whose gender identity is different from their assigned sex at birth.

Questioning: A person in active process of exploring his or her sexual orientation, gender identity, and/or gender conformity. Not all people who question their identities later identify as lesbian, gay, bisexual, or transgender.

There is much to be written about each of these specific populations, but for these purposes, I am limiting the material to the issues faced by LGBTQ students, students whose parents are LGBTQ, and LGBTQ educators within the school context and as encountered by members of the helping professions. There may be few student population groups which raise such controversy or contend with such bias. Students who identify or are identified by others as LGBTQ often face discrimination and challenges in the school. These students are at greater risk for harassment and victimization (Fisher et al., 2008) including hate crimes.

LGBTQ students are at high risk of depression, substance abuse, suicidal ideations and completions, sexual risk taking, poor school achievement and attendance, and dropping out of school (DePaul, Walsh, & Dam, 2009), not because of emotional or mental illness but often because of stress, anxiety, isolation, and fear resulting from treatment by other students and sometimes even by faculty, staff, and administration. Forty-five percent of gay males and 20% of lesbians report having experienced verbal harassment and/or physical violence related to their sexual identity during high school. Ninety-seven percent of all students in public high schools report regularly hearing homophobic remarks from their peers; 53% of students report hearing homophobic comments made by school staff; 80% of prospective teachers report negative attitudes toward gay and lesbian people (LAMBDA, 2009).

Hate crimes are criminal acts motivated by bias and/or hatred of a person or group based upon perceived race, religion, ethnicity, gender, sexual orientation, or other characteristic. Forty-seven states and the District of Columbia have laws against hate crimes. Of those, 29 states have statutes that specifically cover crimes based on the real or perceived sexual orientation of the victim. Seven of those states and the District of Columbia cover gender identity. Nineteen percent of gay/lesbian youth report suffering homophobic physical attacks and 15% have been injured so badly they have had to seek medical services. Twenty percent of LBGTQ youth report skipping school because of feeling unsafe while there. Forty-two percent of adolescent lesbians and 34% of adolescent gay males who have been victims of homophobic violence report attempting suicide (LAMBDA, 2009).

Transgendered students are at even higher risk of harassment, persecution, and physical assaults (gay bashing), including rape. Likewise, rates of depression, anxiety, substance abuse (including intravenous hormones and silicone), and suicidal attempts and completions are extremely high. Self-injury and/or mutilation is a particular problem as is sexual risk taking (Denny, 2009; Parents, Families & Friends of Lesbians and Gays [PFLAG], 2009). PFLAG literature points out that "transgendered people are found in every country, society, and culture from the most primitive to the most advanced" and states, "the evidence suggests that transgenderism is but another facet of the diverse human condition."

Whether a student is lesbian, gay, bisexual, transgendered, or questioning his or her sexual preference/orientation, school counselors can help in a number of ways. Adapted from LAMBDA's *When a Student Tells You They're Gay* (2010) webpage, here are few simple ways to respond if a student comes out to you:

- Be yourself.
- Remember that the student may be afraid.
- Use the vocabulary they use.
- Be aware of your comfort and limitations.
- Do your homework.
- Respect the student's right to privacy and confidentiality.
- Thank the student for trusting you.
- If the student is having trouble with harassment or abuse, follow your school's procedures for filing an incident report and/or reporting violence on campus.

DePaul, Walsh, and Dam (2009) assert that several defining characteristics of school counselors distinguish them as potential leaders in addressing the issues faced by sexual minority students. Among these characteristics are training in child development, systems perspective, and professional commitment to diversity. The authors also note that the current social debate surrounding same-sex rights and public clash of ideologies make it difficult for counselors to raise the awareness and the safety levels within their schools. They propose an action plan which falls along a continuum: (a) whole-school prevention, (b) targeted prevention, and (c) intensive intervention.

This plan echoes the NASP school-based interventions which include the following:

- Improve school safety.
- Dispel misinformation and affirm diversity.
- Provide a support network for sexual minority students.
- Prevent discrimination.
- Ensure sexual minority students equal access to all school-related activities.
- Train all staff members to understand sexual minority students and use effective interventions.

- Be aware and wary of interventions to change an individual's sexual orientation.
- Be prepared to address controversy.

Fisher et al. (2008) suggest (a) primary prevention and intervention strategies of policy development, (b) curriculum development, (c) staff development and schoolwide education, (d) secondary prevention and intervention in the form of support groups, group counseling, and diversity rooms, and (e) tertiary prevention and intervention of maintaining culturally competent practices, treatment planning, and therapeutic (or clinical) process.

A program developed in an alternative high school in Fort Collins, Colorado, is described in an article by Bauman and Sachs-Kapp (1998) who advise it behooves the counselor not only to work individually and/or in groups with students to provide support and acceptance but also to work proactively and systemically to promote a school climate that is safe and nurturing for all students, including LGBTQ students. They concur with DePaul et al. (2009) in stating, " . . . counselors are in a unique position in the schools and, as student advocates, must take a variety of approaches promoting diversity." The Fort Collins program trained, assisted, and supported student leaders and facilitators as a powerful way to make a statement about the school climate and expectations. School counselors were on the forefront of promoting these efforts.

Students whose parents identify as members of a sexual minority face similar yet distinct challenges within the school community. It is not uncommon for harassment and discrimination to occur if the sexual orientation of a student's parent(s) is known. Slurs and hate speech is frequent. Assumptions about the student's sexuality are made, and therefore, they may suffer the same sorts of abuse that LGBTQ students endure.

When the LGBTQ parents are not "out" to the school community, the student may feel isolated by the family "secret." For younger children, this can be especially confusing. For adolescents, it may be a time of distance, rebellion, and loneliness. Using inclusive language, introducing a variety of family types in social studies and health classes, and ensuring the lives and contributions of gays, lesbians, bisexual, and transgendered people are studied in history, art, and sociology classes can greatly increase the comfort level of students who come from sexually diverse households. School counselors may have no control over educational curriculum, but they can educate faculty and administration and advocate for school policies that do provide acceptance and empowerment.

Often, students may fall somewhere in between. It may be well known that the student has two moms or dads, but no one talks about it. Lucian is "parent poor." He has two moms, godfathers, and a whole host of aunts and uncles. Lucian's moms, Sondra and Eileen, had been together for five years when they decided to have a baby. Eileen is white; Sondra is Afro-Cuban. Because they were a biracial couple, Sondra and

Eileen chose a sperm bank and anonymous donor in order to conceive a biracial child.

Lucian attends a progressive school with other students from many diverse family configurations; he doesn't experience the kind of overt harassment many students do, but he is a confused and conflicted young man. He loves his family, and they dote on him, but he isn't sure where his allegiances should be placed. To make matters more confusing for Lucian, Sondra and Eileen separated. Like all children of "divorce," Lucian was sad, depressed, angry, and self-blaming. Because of the uncertainty at his home, Lucian began spending more and more time with his extended family of godfathers, aunts, and uncles. This was stabilizing, but it was also confusing, especially when the dads and uncles began to take Lucian to school or sat in on parent-teacher conferences instead of the moms. The school appropriately secured release forms from Sondra and Eileen, but some of the faculty were disturbed by this new arrangement. They expressed concerns about the relationship between Lucian and the various gay men who played such an important role in his life.

The school counselor, herself a lesbian, was at first offended by the comments made during staff meetings, but she decided to be proactive, not only for Lucian, but for all the sexual minority students, parents, and faculty members. She organized a Gay-Straight Alliance (GSA) at the school and invited the faculty and administration to the first meeting. Prior to the meeting, she identified students with varied experiences and asked for their participation. Lucian was one the students. At first he was reluctant, saying, "But I'm not gay!" but finally agreed when the school counselor explained the premise of a GSA. GSAs are designed to provide safe, supportive environments in which students can meet and talk about issues that affect all students. GSAs are generally student led with the support of a faculty advisor, often the school counselor, social worker, or psychologist (GLESN, 2009). For GSAs to work, it is important that heterosexual students feel comfortable as well; LGBTQ students sometimes must examine their own biases in order to openly engage their straight peers in conversation. Lucian's participation offered valuable information and clarified many things which had otherwise been left to speculation.

Lucian seemed to feel less reluctant to talk about his extensive family, and his general demeanor improved significantly. The concerned faculty found things were much more normal at Lucian's houses than they realized. Rather than viewing him as the son of lesbian or gay parents, they began to see him as a child of divorce, living between two homes while the adults sorted out their own lives. This was something they had seen hundreds of times and had plenty of skills to handle.

As part of her organization of the first GSA meeting, the school counselor took the opportunity and "came out" to her colleagues and students. After seven years on the job, she briefly introduced herself as a school counselor, a pianist at her church, an avid caver, a struggling golfer, and a lesbian. To her delight, most questions from both students and colleagues were about spelunking.

Specific resources, links, and suggested reading including Chaz Bono's books, *Family Outing* and *End of Innocence*, can be found in the Resources section of this book, under "Chapter 7 Resources."

ABSTINENCE AND PURITY

Barb Anderson (2010) of the Minnesota Family Counsel asserts that teenagers who make "purity pledges" to remain sexually abstinent until marriage are 34% less likely to have sex than those who do not make the pledge. She states that the Centers for Disease Control and Prevention confirm teen pregnancy has decreased since the introduction of the concept in 1993, being most effective for 16- and 17-year-olds. The purity and abstinence pledges are also thought to reduce incidents of sexually transmitted disease (STD). Other reports dispute this.

In a study done at Johns Hopkins School of Public Health, data indicated no measurable results, concluding that teens who pledged purity or abstinence were less likely to have premarital sex than other teens who did not pledge virginity. Both groups began having premarital sex at about the same age, had an average of three lifetime partners, and had similar rates of STDs. Unmarried pledgers, however, were less likely to use birth control or condoms, putting them at higher risk of unplanned pregnancy and STDs (Rosenbaum, 2009).

As I put the final touches on this manuscript, a *Washington Post* breaking news article (Stein, 2010) arrived on my Blackberry: "Study Provides Evidence That Abstinence Only Sex Education Can Be Effective." I follow up to find that this study has been conducted by the University of Pennsylvania and has been published in the Archives of Pediatric and Adolescent Medicine. The study, conducted between 2001 and 2004 involved 662 African American students from four public middle schools. This is a relatively small data pool yet significant in that the study meets the criteria for consideration in federal funding for sex education in schools given administration budget cuts which eliminated funding for such programs based on prior inefficiency.

For some students, abstinence and purity pledges are the new cool. For others, these declarations may put them in positions of greater peer pressure, ridicule, or harm. Because there is often a religious base for the decision to remain abstinent, there is also the propensity for religious debate or persecution to erupt. The role of the school counselor is not to advocate for one stance or another but to accept the student's decision and protect him or her from negative remarks or behavior by others. In addition, the school counselor must also make sure that students who do not choose abstinence are not the brunt of proselytizing.

REPRODUCTIVE HEALTH

After declining steadily from 1991 to 2005, birth rates for 15- to 19-year-olds increased significantly; however, this increase was not seen in younger girls. In addition, rates of AIDS among males aged 15 to 24 increased from 1997 to 2006. Cases of syphilis have increased among both males and females ages 15 to 24 in recent years (Centers for Disease Control and Prevention, 2010).

The focus of reproductive health is overwhelming on prevention of teen pregnancy and geared toward girls. This is important but ignores other important issues such as programs targeting males and post-pregnancy solutions to drop-out rates and economic impact.

Nineteen states and the District of Columbia require schools to provide sexuality education. Of these, four states require abstinence education and information about contraception. Thirty-four states and the District of Columbia require schools to provide STD, HIV, and AIDS education.

Although there is widespread disagreement about the topic of teen sexuality, research does seem to show there is a direct link to educational success and/or failure as predictors of teen pregnancy. Delayed sexual intercourse correlates with a strong connection to school and higher educational achievement. Five strategies for schools are suggested by the bipartisan organization, National Campaign to Prevent Teen and Unplanned Pregnancy (2010):

1. Promote educational success and provide an enhanced sense that life holds positive options.

2. Help youth create and maintain strong connections to parents and other adults.

3. Provide knowledge, reinforce positive social norms, and enhance social skills through various types of sex education.

4. Offer contraceptive services or make referrals for them.

5. Carry out multiple approaches through school and community partnerships.

School counselors can play a large role in implementing these strategies.

Nancy Griffin (1998) presented a more positive perspective on adolescent parenthood. In a 1998 article, she described a flexibly funded, adolescent-parent support program that coordinated an array of services aimed at diminishing the limitations placed on the teen-parent life options and promoting optimal development of teen parents and their children. The program objectives included increased teen self-efficacy in the following areas:

1. Planning child spacing and delaying or planning pregnancy

2. Coping with stress of infant and child care

3. Succeeding in academic performance, persistence, and choice

4. Identifying and utilizing community resources and strengthening support systems

5. Obtaining part-time employment

6. Adjusting to the demands of the job

7. Planning and making decisions for the future

Support groups and mother mentors were also program components. In conclusion, Griffin (1998) states,

> In serving each adolescent parent, school counselors are in a unique position to understand the needs of the whole student, to know community resources and gaps in service, to coordinate student and family access to existing services, and to advocate for the development of additional services based on a philosophy that promotes self-efficacy and fosters resiliency. . . . While adherence to a clear, theoretical basis provides consistency for any program that serves this population, the structure must remain student centered and flexible, evolving in response to changing needs and resources of both students and the community.

RISK TAKING

As I perused the research on sexual risk taking among adolescents, I found myself somewhat baffled at the lack of information. My experience of sexual risk taking among teens is not limited to sexual intercourse without birth control or condom. When I consider sexual risk taking, I am concerned about students who are not only having unprotected sex but also are having sex with multiple partners, dangerous partners, and anonymous partners, and engaging in sadomasochistic behavior or prostitution. I don't like to consider these things, but I must because adolescents and yes, some children, are involved in these practices, and they desperately need help.

It is true that a large percentage of these children and adolescents have a sexual trauma history, a drug and/or alcohol abuse history, a history of domestic violence within their homes, or histories of other types of self-harmful acts—but not all. In fact, in my experience, the most vulnerable are those children and teens not having the required self-preservation skills to survive very long in these circumstances.

All too often, I have been in case consultations or supervision with counselors, therapists, and other helpers who may hear students talk about their sexual experiences or see the results of sadistic behavior and choose not to believe such activities occur, especially if the student is a "nice" kid from a "good" home. Often they are thought to be exaggerating or not really knowing what they are talking about. Conversely, I have also witnessed helpers do nothing about sexual violence against teens they are no longer surprised by, as if the student probably "asked for it" or "initiated."

My bachelor's degree was in mass media, and I am a strong proponent of advances in media technology; however, I do recognize that with advances come hazards. Media have made sex and violence nearly interchangeable, and easy access through Internet and wireless devices has given younger and younger children the feeling they can and should be a part of the new age of immediate gratification.

When talking with students, we must make sure we are comfortable with the subject matter. We must do our homework and update our vocabulary so we are seen as current on the issues but also in an effort to avoid making our student clients feel uncomfortable or awkward by having to explain things in graphic detail. School counselors can promote sexual safety, self-care, and responsibility by coordinating efforts with health educators and technology instructors. Having a zero-tolerance policy and clearly including sexual risk taking in a list of risk-taking or dangerous behavior is advised.

CULTURAL CONSIDERATIONS

- Be clear about your own beliefs about sex, sexual practices, preferences, and orientation. The more we know about ourselves, the less likely we are to project onto others. (ASCA National Model Standards—B.1.d., B.2.d., C.1.c., D.2.a., b.)

- Become sexually current. Terms, issues, and options are different than they were 30, 20, 10, even 5 years ago. (ASCA National Model Standards—A.1.a., b., c., A.3.a., b., B.1.a., b., E.1.a., b., c., E.2.a., b., c., d.)

- Continue to create a climate of inclusion in your school community. (ASCA National Model Standards—A.3.b., E.1.a., b., c., E.2.a., b., c., d.)

- Continue to be proactive in enforcement of consequences for exclusion, prejudicial talk, or behavior. Even if you don't understand, agree, or condone a student's sexual choices, it is imperative to protect his or her rights to an education free of bias. (ASCA National Model Standards—E.1.a., b., c., E.2.a., b., c., d., F.1.a., b., d.)

- Respond directly to bigotry or intolerance of other school professionals. If you don't, who will? (ASCA National Model Standards—E.2.a., b., c., d., F.1.a., b., d., F.2.b., c., G.1., 2., 3., 4.)

- Consult agencies or advocacy organizations which have more knowledge about a particular population or behavior. (ASCA National Model Standards—D.1.c., E.1.c., E.2.d., F.2.a., G.1.)

- Advocate the inclusion of LBGTQ people in curriculum. (ASCA National Model Standards—A.3.b., E.1.a., b., c., E.2.a., b., c., d.)

STRATEGIES TO SUPPORT AND FACILITATE CULTURALLY CONSIDERATE COUNSELING

- Assess the overall sexual safety of your school.

- Advocate a zero-tolerance policy of sexual harassment, discrimination, hate speak, or hate crimes within the school.

- Model sexual boundaries in dress, manner, and conversation.

- Have "courageous conversations" about student sexuality with other professionals. Correct misinformation.

- Visit coffee houses, bookstores, and functions owned by or which support sexual minorities.

- Remember the importance of privacy and confidentiality, including sharing information with parents about a student's sexual orientation and practices.

- Show your student client that she or he can trust adults with sensitive information so that he or she may eventually share information with caregivers.

- Provide networking opportunities for sexual minority students and ensure equal access to all school-related activities.

- Provide supportive networks for pregnant girls and prospective teen fathers to encourage school completion.

- Expect controversy and have an action plan in place to address issues that will arise.

CHAPTER SUMMARY

An equitable school environment starts with access but goes beyond. "We've tended to define [gender equitable education] in terms of lega-listic issues . . . [such as] equal access and Title IX, and in reality, that doesn't get at the gender ideologies that are so rampant throughout the system . . ." (Bailey, 2001). Bailey goes on to state, " . . . I don't think we've made too much progress in really addressing how it feels for kids in schools."

On the elementary school level, Thorne (2001) recommends challenging the kind of gender separation of girls against boys. Some practices may feed this, but others lessen division and promote cooperation and friendship between girls and boys.

Educators must observe and respond to behaviors and learning progress of boys and girls as groups then fine-tune teaching styles and pedagogy to ensure that learning occurs for all. Some research has identified cooperative and collaborative learning as especially effective and conducive for female students in math and sciences, while other research on boys has emphasized that some kinds of reading material or long periods of immobility may alienate boys from school. Participants emphasized that given the rich body of literature on effective teaching styles, teachers should be equipped to use a variety of techniques to suit particular dynamics of the classroom and ensure equal engagement in learning by diverse boys and girls. Successful and equitable schools will encourage equal academic achievement and engagement for boys and girls across the curriculum and will also equip them to live and work together in an increasingly diverse society (AAUW Education Foundation, 2001).

My shift from working for the rights of women and girls to working for the rights of all those held back because of or held accountable to their gender roles came first when I was still working in the agency for battered women and rape survivors. I began to see a few men who were referred by female friends. Often, they were gay men who needed a safe place to talk about partner violence. Others were male rape survivors.

Nothing, however, showed me the true necessity of gender equity like counseling very young boys. I watched them struggle from within, mirror images of the girls I treated years earlier, frustrated when they weren't good at sports, when they didn't conform to gender role ideals, when they were too scared to fight back when harassed by the school bully, and when they grieved for fathers who had sexually violated them.

As professional helpers, we like to think of ourselves as open-minded, accepting, and capable of putting our own value system aside for the sake of our clients. As caring adults, we don't like to think of children in sexual circumstances of any kind. We seldom think kids should be having kids of their own. There are many topics that push buttons, however. Sexuality and sexual orientation are among those that push most frequently and push back with most vehemence.

Many of those belonging to the "greatest generation" were born to teen mothers and often teen fathers. Things are different now, and that no longer is a societal norm, but we forget that if our adolescents possess the biology to become parents, they also possess the innate wisdom to parent properly. The mothers of the greatest generation no doubt relied on family and community support to raise children who became heroes to a nation. We must re-create social, community, and school systems that allow teen mothers and fathers to finish their education and promote hope for their futures rather than assuming they will never complete high school let alone higher education.

Recently, Congress began hearings on ending the awkward "Don't Ask, Don't Tell" policy on gays and lesbians in the military. The highest governing officers have come to realize the waste of time and human resources this policy has caused for already overworked armed forces and have begun to advocate for its cessation. This attitudinal shift, fueled by pragmatism, is a signal for us all to look beyond our bias and become cognizant of what our LBGTQ students have to offer. If the joint chiefs can do it, surely we can do it.

PART II

Interfacing With Family, Faculty, Administration, and Community

8

School-Family-Community Partnerships

R esearch is finally indicating what educators have known for years: family involvement in school increases school achievement and student confidence. Over the past decade, school counselors have been at the forefront of developing and implementing school-family partnerships. In school counseling programs where social justice is a priority, school counselors recognize the benefits of school-family-community (SFC) partnerships and spend a good deal of time working with parents and community-based organizations (Holcomb-McCoy, 2007). There is no question of the benefit of parental involvement, though parents of culturally and linguistically diverse students continue to avoid participation in the school system, and schools very often assume this is due to parental disinterest instead of addressing barriers that cause them to be uninvolved (Martines, 2008).

In many schools, efforts to include family and community in student education may be uncoordinated or unsupported. As a result, school, family, and community partnerships may be built on trial and error rather than as a part of an organized strategy to meet student goals. Inequities in family and community involvement matter for students (Sheldon, 2007). Factors likely to influence the extent to which families become involved include parent beliefs, socioeconomic status, parents' own school experiences, and cultural considerations. The National Network of Partnership Schools (NNPS) provides member schools with tools and guidelines for establishing, maintaining, and improving schoolwide partnership programs that reach out to the families of all students. Utilizing Epstein et al.'s (2002) framework, the NNPS advocates six types of involvement to create comprehensive SFC partnerships:

1. Helping families establish supportive home environments

2. Establishing two-way exchanges about school programs and children's progress

3. Recruiting and organizing parent help at school, home, or other locations

4. Providing ideas to families about how to help students with homework and other curriculum-related materials

5. Having family members serve as representatives and leaders on school committees

6. Identifying and integrating resources and services from the community to strengthen school programs

NNPS also encourages schools to examine their partnership practices and ensure families from all racial, ethnic, and educational backgrounds are provided information in words and forms they understand; provide alternative locations for parental volunteer opportunities; and include parents who represent various groups on school decision-making boards and committees (Sheldon, 2007).

Holcomb-McCoy (2007) states the three primary roles of the school:

1. Giving parents access to information and skills to support their children's education

2. Coordinating community programming that meets the needs and issues that students and their families encounter

3. Recognize the rights of parents—and their fundamental competence—to share in decision making

Nahari (Martines, 2008) cites Blue-Banning and colleagues in identifying six categories of themes crucial for successful parental involvement programs: communication, commitment, equality, skills, trust, and respect. Nahari (Martines, 2008) further advocates the adoption of a "posture of reciprocity" via Kalyanpur and Harry (Martines, 2008) and presents the following suggestions for establishment and maintenance of parental involvement with multicultural considerations:

1. Create reliable systems of communications.

2. Implement services that support parent participation.

3. Educate parents regarding the U.S. school system and culture.

Families have a variety of reasons for not becoming involved in schools which range from inconvenient meeting times to feeling unwelcome in the school. Creative planning to overcoming barriers for parents is essential to social justice focused school counseling programs (Holcomb-McCoy, 2007). Holcomb-McCoy also asserts counselors and other educators are often resistant to developing closer relationships with parents as well as with community members, often citing time constraints and workload as reasons.

School counselors are likely to have a positive impact on at risk clients when they refer to and consult with other providers and programs in the communities. Wraparound service programs provide opportunities to develop formal and informal support networks for at risk youth in an individualized and coordinated setting. This type of service also draws on the strengths of family and cultural resources (Fusick & Bordeau, 2006). Truly, successful schools extend invitations to the community to participate and keep the community fully informed on school activities, progress, and performance providing experiences, ideas, and financial and material resources (Holcomb-McCoy, 2007).

When selecting individuals, agencies, or organizations for SFC committees, Holcomb-McCoy (2007) suggests the following criteria:

1. Identify and involve people whose support is absolutely critical such as the school principal.

2 Identify influential community leaders.

3. Identify members from diverse backgrounds.

4. Find people who have a strong interest in helping the school and community.

5. Involve members whose positions, expertise, and skills match the initiative.

Resources for these initiatives include religious and spiritual leaders, community leaders and professionals, and representatives from culturally distinct colleges and universities (Martines, 2008). In some cultures, traditional healers are extremely important in the health and cohesiveness of efforts to bring schools, families, and community together (Moodley & West, 2005).

Bryan and Holcomb-McCoy (2004) present an extensive review of the literature which reveals nine SFC partnership programs frequently found in schools:

1. Mentoring Programs

2. Parent Centers

3. Family and Community Members as Teachers' Aides

4. Parent and Community Volunteer Programs

5. Home Visit Programs

6. Parent Education Programs

7. School-Business Partnerships

8. Parents and Community Member in Site-Based Management

9. Tutoring Programs

Bryan and Holcomb-McCoy further identify the role of school counselors as having potential for leadership in promoting educational reform through SFC partnerships.

Bryan and Henry (2008) state, "Good counseling and education recognize and build strengths rather than focus on problem reduction and correction" (p. 149). They urge SFC partnerships to be strength based, utilizing the assets found in schools, families, and communities to create strength-enhancing environments which promote caring and positive adult-child relationships, strengthen student social support networks, foster academic success, and empower students with a sense of purpose: "Rather than pathologizing families and children of color, school personnel should affirm families' efforts and collaborate with family and community members and organizations to provide the extra-family support [needed] to overcome the numerous challenges they face" (p. 149).

Bryan and Henry (2008) assert that school counselors are in an ideal position to promote a strength-based approach throughout the school by highlighting the importance of student and family strengths, promoting a language of strength throughout the school, reframing the way adults talk about children, showing respect for student and family struggles, and emphasizing strengths development schoolwide. They state SFC partnerships are especially conducive for building strength-enhancing environments which promote protective factors, developmental assets, and resources in order to increase resiliency in children, opportunities for meaningful student participation in school and community, and high parent and teacher expectations. These factors produce empowerment and support externally while encouraging a commitment to learning, positive values and identity, and social competencies.

Examples of SFC partnerships which benefit the needs of families of specific cultural groups are presented by Dotson-Blake, Foster, and Gressard (2009) and by Mitchell and Bryan (2007). Dotson-Blake and colleagues explored SFC partnerships to engage Latino (specifically Mexican) immigrant families while Mitchell and Bryan presented challenges faced by immigrants from Caribbean countries.

Dotson-Blake et al. (2009) cite conflicting values between home and school, socioeconomics, language, acculturation, and immigration status as factors influencing students and their families who immigrate to the United States from Mexico. Mexican children often enter the American educational system with hopeful and high expectations. They carry an inherent tradition of respect for and identification with both nuclear and extended family. Their collective worldview includes cohesiveness and interdependence and may be quickly confused and conflicted by their new educational environment in which independence and individualism are valued and reinforced in the classroom.

Mexican parents often accept employment requiring little exposure to English, while their children are immersed in English on a daily basis. Children become adept with new language more quickly than adults and may even lose some of their own native language, creating a gap not only in functional communication but in emotional language as well. Similarly, acculturation rates between parents and children can be quite different and cause further division and isolation. Adding to these stressors, immigration status can impact families and children in a myriad of ways which affect not only school performance but also day-to-day feelings of safety and security.

Dotson-Blake and colleagues (2009) state that cultural discontinuity between the ethnicity of school personnel and the families in the community may lead to family perceptions that their cultural values are not accepted or valued by the school. Dotson-Blake and colleagues, like other authors, perceive school counselors as essential to effective SFC partnerships. They propose the following template for partnerships with Mexican immigrant families:

1. Foster Respect and Culture of Equal Engagement

2. Create a Welcoming, Collaborative Climate

3. Identify Cultural Brokers and Community Leaders

4. Plan Intentional, Structured Opportunities to Interact

5. Bolster Investment Through Community Engagement and Reciprocity

6. Reflect on the Success and Effectiveness of Partnership Efforts

Family-school-community partnerships in Mexico are structured in such a manner as to benefit all stakeholders equally, the success of the family being central to the effective education of children. Success of each family, in turn, is viewed as key to community success.

Mitchell and Bryan (2007) write,

Several authors have attributed the high dropout rate among Caribbean immigrant students to the negative experiences they have within public schools in the United States. Caribbean parents and children typically do not receive adequate, culturally competent counseling services, which affects their academic outcomes and ultimately limits their life chances. (p. 399)

Caribbean parents are often unaware of the need to closely monitor their child's experience because they come from a culture in which the school acts in tandem with parents.

Immigrants from the Caribbean are an extremely diverse population, which includes influences from Africa, Spain, Britain, France, Holland, Asia, and American Indian cultures. While immigrants from the Caribbean often share a common set of cultural values, specific language and customs may be quite varied. Collectivism, the importance of spirituality, self-enhancement, and strong sense of ethnic pride and history are characteristics. Understanding concepts of family, including "fictive kin" and the multiethnic and linguistic heritage are essential to supportive services to these families.

Issues often impacting Caribbean immigrant families are economic stressors, familial separation due to migration patterns, language, and acculturative stress. Mitchell and Bryan (2007) likewise cite Epstein's six-item typology of partnership involvement adapted by the National Parent-Teacher Association as useful interventions for Caribbean families involved in SFC partnerships. In addition, they advise establishment of home visit programs and parent centers as a means of reaching and involving more families and collaborating with volunteers of Caribbean ethnicity. Mitchell and Bryan also recognize the important role school counselors play in SFC partnerships and encourage counselors to voice the needs of the Caribbean families of their schools and mobilize community resources to help meet those needs, some of which include school-to-work transition programs, faith-based organizations for character and moral influence, and local colleges and universities for tutoring and mentoring programs. Holcomb-McCoy (2007) further asserts the importance of identifying parent leaders who emerge and what strategies have worked to develop more diverse parent and community participation.

CULTURAL CONSIDERATIONS

- Listen carefully to parents and community leaders; ask questions; never assume. (ASCA National Model Standards—A.1.a., b., c., A.3.a., b., B.1.a., b., D.1.a.,b., c., g., D.2.a., b., E.1.a., b., c., E.2.a., b., c., d.)

- Create a climate of inclusion and interest within and outside of the school community. (ASCA National Model Standards—A.3.b., D.1.a., b., c., g., D.2.a., b., E.1.a., b., c., E.2.a., b., c., d.)

- Respond swiftly and directly to bigotry or intolerance during meetings. (ASCA National Model Standards—D.1.a., b., c., g., D.2.a., b., E.2.a., b., c., d., F.1.a., b., d., F.2.b., c., G.1., 2., 3., 4.)

- Invite colleagues who may have more personal or professional experience with a particular population to be a part of the committee. (ASCA National Model Standards—C.1.a., b., c., C.2.a., b., c., d., D.1.c., E.1.c., E.2.d., F.2.a., G.1.)

- Attend professional workshops, presentations, and conferences to expand cultural awareness and competency. (ASCA National Model Standards—E.1.c., E.2.d., G.1., 2., 3., 4.)

STRATEGIES TO SUPPORT AND FACILITATE CULTURALLY CONSIDERATE COUNSELING

- Be flexible about meeting times. Take into account cultural norms, accessibility, and religious practices when setting dates and locations.

- Communicate in as many ways as possible. Ask for help from bilingual colleagues or community leaders when needed.

- Arrange transportation and provide childcare if possible.

- Encourage expression and never silence or discount a parent's perspective.

- Solicit advice from parents on what might work better.

- Invite community leaders into the school during school time so they may be exposed to the same atmosphere as students and their families.

- Be aware of school programs which may not be inclusive and suggest alternatives.

- When planning luncheons or meetings which might include food, be conscientious of culture-based or ability-based dietary requirements.

CHAPTER SUMMARY

In evaluating school-family-community partnerships, both quantitative and qualitative methods should be used including interviews, focus groups, and surveys in order to assess progress of school initiatives and make adjustments where needed. According to Bryan and Henry (2008), students are either empowered or disempowered by their relationships with adults in schools. Empowerment gives children skills and knowledge necessary to succeed, feel valued and included in the school, and develop a sense of purpose and confidence. In schools where children of color or those from lower income circumstances are empowered, adults believe and implement a variety of practices that contribute to such empowerment. These adults have high expectations for all students and believe success is possible. They value the culture and the language of students, treat both students and parents with respect and care, recognize families as valuable assets and powerful allies, and believe the school exists to serve families and community. They foster a nurturing and positive environment for students and a warm, welcoming climate for parents.

9

Team Building

Experts agree that establishing meaningful connections between teachers and students in the classroom is an essential part of educational success. Educators realize when schools attend to students' social and emotional needs, academic achievement increases, problem behaviors decrease, and quality of the relations surrounding each child improves. The influence and expectations of principals, their understanding of the role of the school counselor, and implementation of effective school guidance and counseling programs are also influential in recognizing the importance of school counselors in support of students, teachers, and the school as a whole (Clark & Amatea, 2004).

Collaboration with all those involved in the education of our student clients is essential to provide the best services with the most efficacious outcomes. Team building can be sensitive, tedious, and tiresome in some settings. In others, team building is a natural outgrowth of a positive, well-trained, and motivated administration. In both circumstances, school counselors are in central positions and often poised to be leaders in initiating and maintaining cohesive professional teams.

Sink and Edwards (2008) cite Gardner and Bruner when calling for schools to be conceptualized as "learning communities" or "schools as communities" which are based upon developing a strengths-based school culture and environment. Further citing literature from related helping professions, they advocate for collaboration with and learning from all members of the community to provide the best possible atmosphere for students. Sink and Edwards (2008) state, "Perhaps central to creating and maintaining CCLs (Caring Community of Learning) is the importance of providing culturally appropriate services and assessing the resiliency, strengths, and protective factors of students" (p. 111).

FACULTY

Clark and Amatea (2004) identified the following themes in team building and collaboration between school counselors and teachers: building positive relationships and communication, counselor visibility, informing teachers about the role and contribution of the school counselor, viewing classrooms and schools as systems.

Another extremely important factor in building peer relationships, which lead to fruitful collaboration on behalf of students, is school counselors' respect and value of teachers as first point of contact. Many school counselors have been teachers; many have not. Regardless, seeking the perspective of a student client's classroom teacher(s) is critical to forming insight about the student and fosters good will and rapport with faculty members. Teachers may not be trained in counseling methods or techniques, but they are trained to assess students, and they are in positions to see students in multiple situations, eliciting a variety of responses. Faculty also often have a better understanding of the school as organism and how the organism may contribute to the individual student's current or ongoing needs.

The American School Counselor Association (ASCA) National Model recommends counselors collaborate with teachers to present "proactive, prevention-based guidance curriculum lessons" (2005). School counselors can facilitate discussions and workshops for educators to explore their own cultural stereotypes and expectations for minority status students (Fusick & Bordeau, 2006).

Ponterotto, Mendelowitz, and Collabolletta (2008) suggest the importance of helping professionals seeking the consultation of multicultural and minority leaders in the school. Because the number of faculty is generally larger than other groups of school professionals, finding these leaders among teachers is most likely. Martines (2008) echoes this in writing, "Multicultural consultation competency includes the facility to consult successfully with teachers of various ethnic backgrounds" (p. 279).

ADMINISTRATION

Research demonstrates discrepancies between professional school counselors' role and principals' perceptions of appropriate tasks, time spent on tasks, and the basic role of the counselor. These discrepancies have a major influence on the relationship with school counselors and principals, counselors and faculty, and the overall environment of schools. The effectiveness of a school counseling program is determined largely by the school leaders, yet principals do not readily understand the counselor's role or potential impact as a leader within the school (Leuwerke, Walker, & Qi, 2009).

The counselor-principal relationship may be impacted by the growing number of mandates and school reform initiatives focusing on accountability, student achievement, and equity. Declining budgets, managerial relations, and increasingly complicated legal issues often interfere with a principal's ability to address daily running of the school. The effectiveness of coordinated efforts of the school counselor and the school principal is a decisive factor for school reform, and counselors find their jobs difficult when there is a lack of support from the principal.

Leuwerke et al. (2009) cite a number of factors that encourage a positive, supportive relationship between principals and school counselors. Principals value counselors who are able to problem solve, advocate on behalf of students, and effect change in the school. The relationship is strengthened significantly when a clear definition of the counselor's role is understood and respected by both parties. When professional school counselors feel adequately supported and are assigned appropriate duties, they report increased career satisfaction and commitment. Even brief exposure to the ASCA National Model significantly impacts principals' perception of school counseling and more appropriate expectations.

A study of school social workers and administration found there were similar discrepancies between the two groups in views and understanding of actual services performed by school social workers, although both viewed provision of frontline mental health services as a major benefit. One administrator stated the school social worker, " . . . assists in student emotional health so that more effective learning can take place," and another stated, " . . . problems [are] solved at a building level rather than district level" (Bye, Shepard, Partridge, & Alvarez, 2009, p. 102).

As with school counselors, both administrators and helping professionals indicated an increase of school attendance and decrease in discipline problems were the most expected (and productive) outcomes of social work services, although administrators did not know how outcomes were being reported. Bye et al. (2009) assert that for helping professions to be sustained, the school organization must value and understand the service outcomes and benefits of the work. Differences in expectations between administrators and helping professionals may lead schools to under invest in these services.

"Professional school counselors must be equipped with the necessary tools to collaborate with administrators in assessing how well policies, programs, and practices align with the needs of diverse groups and prepare students to interact globally" (Nelson & Bustamante, 2009).

Nelson and Bustamante advocate the following collaborative practices for improving the cultural proficiency of their school setting:

1. Partner with the principal to be the leaders in assessing school-wide cultural competence.

2. Identify a diverse team of teacher leaders and other stakeholders to assist in the assessment.

3. Use a research instrument such as the SCCOC (Schoolwide Cultural Competence Observation Checklist) to determine strength and need areas in schoolwide cultural competence.

4. Include activities to address the cultural competence need areas of the school.

5. Become knowledgeable about racial identity development and include this knowledge through guidance lessons and staff development.

6. Model cultural competence and challenge inequitable organizational policies and practices.

OTHER PROFESSIONALS AND ADJUNCT RESOURCES

A culturally competent school is one that is successful in both meeting the challenges and seizing the opportunities associated with multiculturalism and diversity (Simcox, Nuijens, & Lee, 2006). In order for this to take place, it is imperative for all educational professionals to be a part of the process. Professional school counselors, school social workers, and school psychologists have similar yet distinct roles in promoting the academic, social, and emotional development of children. Working as collaborative partners, they are in ideal positions to promote culturally competent, high achieving schools. Research has stressed the significance of unifying counseling and psychological services in order to address the growing demand of inclusive education. Simcox et al. (2006) explored a model of collaboration specifically targeted at promoting culturally competent schools.

The model presented by Simcox and colleagues (2006) includes four primary levels of service: Student-Centered Interventions, Family Empowerment, Collegial Collaboration, and Brokering Community Resources. The model expands on previous ideas and offers new directions in promoting collaboration between school professionals and models for students and educators alike, the skills and outcomes of working through the challenges presented by difference: different agendas and differing opinions.

CULTURAL CONSIDERATIONS

- Be open to the ideas of colleagues, especially those who are culturally different from you. (ASCA National Model Standards—A.1.a., b., c., A.3.a., b., B.1.a. b., E.1.a., b., c., C.1.a., b., c., C.2.a., b., c., d., E.2.a., b., c., d.)

- Create a climate of inclusion and interest within both formal and informal meetings. (ASCA National Model Standards—A.3.b., E.1.a., b., c., C.1.a., b., c., C.2.a., b., c., d., E.2.a., b., c., d.)

- Respond swiftly and directly to bigotry or intolerance during staff meetings, luncheons, or staff development sessions. (ASCA National Model Standards—C.1.a., b., c., C.2.a., b., c., d., E.2.a., b., c., d., F.1.a., b., d., F.2.b., c., G.1., 2., 3., 4.)

- Get to know colleagues who are different from you. Show interest in who they are outside of school as well as within. (ASCA National Model Standards—C.1.a., b., c., C.2.a., b., c., d., D.1.c., E.1.c., E.2.d., F.2.a., G.1.)

- When attending professional workshops, presentations, and conferences to expand cultural and awareness and competency, sit next to someone you would ordinarily avoid or join a small group discussion which includes people of various cultures. (ASCA National Model Standards—C.1.a., b., c., C.2.a., b., c., d., E.1.c., E.2.d., G.1., 2., 3., 4.)

STRATEGIES TO SUPPORT AND FACILITATE CULTURALLY CONSIDERATE COUNSELING

- Take into account cultural norms and religious practices when setting dates and times for meetings or staff development.

- Encourage open expression and divergent perspectives.

- Be aware of professional development and in-services which may not be inclusive and suggest alternatives.

- When planning luncheons or meetings which might include food, be conscientious of culture-based or ability-based dietary requirements.

- Develop a better understanding of the challenges of the teachers in your school. Observe not as a school counselor but from a classroom teacher's point of view. Even if you have been in the classroom, each school and each group of students is different.

- Similarly, spend a day in the principal's office. Become familiar with what she or he does on a daily basis. Discover ways in which you might lighten his or her load.

- Be courteous to and inclusive of paraprofessional staff members. They usually know a great deal about what goes on in a school and will gladly share information if asked.

CHAPTER SUMMARY

The executive summary of the ASCA National Model states, "Although school counselors are team players who understand fair-share responsibilities within a school system, they cannot be fully effective when taken away from essential counseling tasks to perform non-counseling activities such as scheduling, testing, classroom coverage, discipline, and clerical responsibilities" (2005).

In delegation of tasks to school counselors, building principals frequently request counselors perform duties not aligned to ASCA standards. Research strongly supports the hypothesis that principals have either not been exposed at all to the ASCA model or rarely exposed (Leuwerke et al., 2009). Professional school counselors and other helpers will always be the strongest advocates for their profession. Professional helpers are encouraged to develop routine, regular communication with principals using multiple resources to better inform principals about their role and activities. Consistent communication and emphasizing outcome-oriented information should greatly enhance counselors' relationship with faculty, administration, and other school personnel.

PART III

School Counseling in the Age of Change

10

Consider These Counseling Challenges

ELEMENTARY SCHOOL

Madison began counseling after the violent murder of her Play Auntie. She was five years old, tall and slim, sweet, funny, polite, well-spoken, and very light skinned. Her mother, Gloria, was a professional woman who took pride in her work, her church, and her daughter.

Madison was able to come to terms with her trauma issues in an appropriate time period. She was less symptomatic, had less anxiety and fewer nightmares, and was beginning to thrive. Things changed when she started first grade and by winter break, her anxiety was back, her nightmares had returned, and in addition, her attitude and behavior had dramatically declined.

Eventually, Madison told her story in the only way she knew. She began to throw fits around clothing, hairstyles, and food. She also began to hit herself. Through art therapy, she drew two Madisons—one good, one bad. The good Madison had a white body with straight hair and "talked right." The other had a light brown body and braids, and "was ghetto." She was clear: the bad Madison was accepted by the other girls. The good Madison was the object of criticism and ridicule. "They say I talk white and ask why my momma doesn't fix my hair. They say boys don't like me 'cause I'm skinny."

During consultation, her mother viewed this artwork and burst out crying, saying, "I went through the same thing when I was her age."

Having placed Madison in a progressive, integrated city school, Gloria had assumed things would be different for her daughter. Gloria was at a loss as to how to help her daughter, stating, "She shouldn't be paying a price for speaking properly or the fact that I don't think it's right to put extensions in her hair."

Madison's challenge was in the duality of her life. Adults considered her "cute," well-mannered, and precocious. Conversely, at home and at school, Madison's behavior was unacceptable. She found no comfort in her peer group who thought her to be "uppity" and mean. She was accused of "acting white" and told she had "bad hair."

After several months of little progress, Madison was referred for a general medical consult in order to rule out any potential problems. It was discovered that Madison suffered from precocious puberty and an extenuating growth condition, both of which contributed to her tallness, low body weight, mood swings, and lack of impulse control. In her family of origin, medical reasons for unruly behaviors were never considered. As she stabilized on appropriate medications, Madison was better able to control her mood, impulses, and behaviors. In addition to performing better in school, she was able to develop better peer relationships.

Madison's mother, Gloria, also began to feel less anxious, less responsible for her daughter's unhappiness, and less frustrated with the African American children at school. Slowly, Gloria allowed Madison to try new hair styles and select some clothes that were less conservative, and tried not to correct or criticize Madison when she used basic slang.

◆ ◆ ◆

Before starting the first grade, Stuart had decided school was not for him. Stuart didn't want to go to school, he didn't like school, and he felt strongly he was needed at home. His mom, a single parent who worked at a coffee house chain so she could provide insurance for her sons, was tired, frustrated, and worried. She had moved from Louisiana where she had been studying premed to escape the abuse of her ex-husband who was now in jail for drug distribution. She had no family and few friends in her new city. She was reliant upon school to take care of her boys. When Stuart didn't go to school, she didn't work.

When Stuart did go to school, it was an event. He had to wear the same pair of pants, the same tennis shoes, and one of two shirts. On special days, he wore a clip-on tie. Stuart also insisted on wearing glasses although he didn't need them, and he carried an old briefcase of his father's instead of a backpack. Needless to say, this drew fire from his peers even in the first grade, but his mother feared what would be in store for Stuart as he got older. Stuart was quite philosophical about it, however. "The other kids probably don't understand, but that's alright. It's what I need if I have to go to school."

Of more concern than his personal dress code or his curious speech patterns was his need to involve himself in anything mechanical, particularly anything with a rotary. Stuart would be sitting quietly in class one minute and be gone the next. Often, he would be escorted to the principal's office by the maintenance man. The next stop was the counseling office. Wide-eyed, Stuart would become very anxious, walking in circles around the room. He would repeatedly say he needed to help with the vacuum. "It just doesn't sound right."

Stuart's mother reported that he was quite the encyclopedia when it came to vacuums. He, in fact, had several at home. He also knew a lot about tornados. "I don't like hurricanes, though," he said. "There are too many variables."

Counseling and art therapy helped Stuart to articulate his fascination with vacuums and tornados. Often, he would draw himself in the middle of a dark tornado and would state, "That's how I feel," before he abruptly got up from the drawing table and paced the room. At times of extreme anxiety, he would jump up and walk in rapid circles, saying, "I've got to suck it up," something his father had said to him often when he would display his eccentric behaviors. It took months before he could tell me why he thought he had to fix all the vacuums in the world and suck it up. "Because then my dad will come back and love me again."

Stuart's official assessment and eventual diagnosis of Asperger syndrome was delayed due his mother's work schedule. When he was finally evaluated by a child psychiatrist specializing in pervasive developmental (autistic spectrum) disorders, Stuart was prescribed medication which did not eradicate the cause but did alleviate many of the symptoms. With diagnosis, Stuart also qualified for special education services which, along with continued counseling, helped him with behavior, impulse control, and concentration.

MIDDLE SCHOOL

The school nurse referred Jasmine for counseling after finding bruises that led to child services temporarily placing her with her paternal grandparents for safekeeping. Jasmine had been acting out in class, stealing from the teacher, and using racial slurs on the playground.

Jasmine was pleasant enough in counseling sessions but was not interested in talking about much other than reality stars. She was nearly fixated on Paris Hilton and Kim Kardashian. At times, it was difficult not to inadvertently encourage her spot-on, fashion week catwalk. After a few weeks of getting to know Paris better than Jasmine, I asked her parents to come in to see me.

Jasmine's mother was Chinese and divorced from her father who was African American. He was in the air force. Jasmine had a younger sister.

Her mother had recently married a man from Mexico, and they also had one daughter together.

In visiting with Jasmine's mother, I found her to be a calm and conscientious parent. Her current husband was courteous and forthcoming, and he appeared appropriate with his own toddler and the middle stepdaughter. When it came to Jasmine, they were hesitant. I bluntly asked what Mrs. Hernandez thought the problem was.

"She is a devil child," her mother plainly said. I asked her to elaborate. "She was born a devil child just like her father. A black devil child."

I pushed a little, knowing Jasmine's sister, Jade. "But doesn't Jade have the same father?"

"Yes, but she isn't black." She pulled a photograph out of her purse. "See?"

Mrs. Hernandez wanted me to see there was a distinct difference in the skin color and features of her daughters. Mr. Hernandez remained silent. He did not necessarily agree with his wife's assessment but was not going to show disrespect by contradicting her.

As distressing as this information was, I was able to use it to draw Jasmine out. Eventually, she came to understand she was treating her classmates as she was treated at home. With help from her teacher, a series of incentives were put in place. If Jasmine succeeded in treating her classmates respectfully, she would be allowed to participate in the Winter Talent Show. When it came time for rehearsals to begin, Jasmine chose to be the student director rather than one of the stars feeling her "expertise" would be more helpful.

I also referred the Hernandez family to family therapy. In authorized consultation with the therapist, I discovered Mrs. Hernandez was slowly coming to terms with her racism and eventually would be able to admit her internalized guilt for marrying outside the Chinese culture.

HIGH SCHOOL

Joseph was an African American adolescent with chronic mental illness and developmental delays. As with many people who experience periodic psychosis, Joseph's delusions tell a story. Each time I met with him, Joseph wanted reassurance. He wanted to make sure that when we die, we will come back "whole." When I asked what he meant, Joseph referred to my scars and to his black skin. "You'll come back without those scars, won't you? And I'll come back as a smart white boy. Ain't that right?"

Each time he asked, I responded by asking, "What do you think, Joseph?"

"Yes, ma'am. I think we'll both come back whole."

I wanted very much to tell Joseph we were both already whole, but he would know that was untrue. He would think I was the one who was "crazy" because beneath his uncomplicated intellect and the protection of his illness, he recognized reality better than most. I would have violated his trust by lying to him, and our alliance, based on honesty and respect, would dissolve.

At the core of our work, the trust of our clients and our own personal and professional integrity is really all we have. Joseph's existential question, "Will I be whole?" is one which has both fascinated and eluded scholars and philosophers for centuries. In his world of limitations, limitless possibilities emerged. Because he had so few mores or inhibitions to govern him, he challenged those around him by truly considering a whole or "Re-Created Life" (Davis, 2009). Joining him in this possibility makes him happy. When happy, Joseph was able to make healthier choices and progress in school.

CONSIDER YOUR CURRENT CASE LOAD

Consider your school counseling clients. Consider how they arrived at your office. Think about their heritage and history, geographic origins, circumstances and situations, affinity or relational bonds. Reconsider how you might see them differently today than you did when they left your office the last time. What would be the same and what would you change in the way you counseled them? If you answer "nothing" to the last question, please think again and read on.

PART IV

*School Counselors
as Change Agents:
Opportunities for Growth*

11

Expanding Clinical Skills

I n *The Biracial and Multiracial Student Experience: A Journey to Racial Literacy* (Davis, 2009), I describe a three-tiered model adapted from a model of Wholistic Practice I developed many years ago as a clinical teaching tool. I witness three distinct planes in all clinical (counseling) relationships, no matter how brief: the Here and Now, the Real World, and the Re-Created Life.

The Here and Now is about what happens during each meeting; in educational terms, it might be called a "teachable moment." The Real World is outside the school counseling office. The Real World is in the classroom, on the playground, and at home, and it includes what a student client takes with him into those other spaces. The Re-Created Life encompasses all a student client becomes as a result of his time in counseling.

This way of viewing the counseling relationship and process can help us to remember each moment counts. In, out, and beyond our individual encounter with students, what happens in our offices, even in the hallways, matters and creates change in them and within us.

In Chapter 12, I share a complete schema of professional development based on an equity model developed by Dr. Bonnie Davis and I (2008), but in preparation for the next section, I suggest three simple "Cs" of Culturally Considerate Counseling:

- *Caution: When in doubt, don't.* Don't speak, don't act, and don't come to any conclusions about how to proceed until you've considered the next two Cs.

- *Conscientiousness.* Listen and learn from your students, their families, colleagues, and allied professionals. An important part of conscientiousness is gratitude. Let your students know you have learned from them. Thank them.
- *Clarity.* Take a step back and inventory thoughts, feelings, and beliefs. Being clear about these things will lead not only to better understanding of ourselves but also to better understanding and acceptance of others.

CURRENT TRENDS

When discussing current trends in school counseling, it is useful to reference trends in education and trends in child and adolescent counseling and/or therapy. These two disciplines may be distinct, but for school counselors, they are by no means mutually exclusive.

Current trends in education lean toward new ways to understand student achievement—or perhaps more accurately, *under*achievement. Alternative assessment, brain research, inclusion, learning styles, English language learning, technology, and closing the achievement gap are among the topics often offered in staff development settings. In child and adolescent therapy circles, current topics often focus on causation of behaviors. Attention deficit/hyperactivity disorders, pervasive developmental disorders (also known as autism spectrum disorders), oppositional defiant disorder, attachment disorders, and bipolar disorder are among the most frequently offered continuing education workshops for practitioners. Somewhere between bullying and school violence, disaster preparedness, character education and service learning, and multicultural and equity education make up many in-service and conference hours.

Christopher Sink, veteran professor of counselor education at Seattle Pacific University and past editor of *Professional School Counseling,* the journal of the American School Counselor Association (Sink, 2010), lists the following trends as key areas for school counselors: student spirituality and meaning making, positive psychology, and strengths-based education and counseling, such as Positive Behavior Support (PBS) and Response to Intervention (RTI), creating schools that are caring learning communities, program evaluation, research methods for accountability leadership.

PBS and RTI are two trends rapidly developing throughout education. PBS includes both systemic and individualized strategies that incorporate managed classrooms and other school areas using a three-tiered approach. Primary, secondary, and tertiary prevention strategies implemented across three school-based levels—nonclassroom, classroom, and individual students—are designed to create a positive school climate (Sherrod, Getch, & Ziomek-Daigle, 2009). RTI is a multitiered problem-solving approach that addresses the learning difficulties by providing educators with guidance on how to match student needs with appropriate levels of support to ensure positive outcomes and foster continued progress (Jackson, Pretti-Frontczak, Harjusola-Webb, Grisham-Brown, & Romani, 2009). Initially, RTI models addressed issues related to children with identified learning disabilities, the term "response to intervention" first appearing in school psychology and special education literature with the initiation of the Individuals with Disabilities Education Act (IDEA), requiring the development of IEPs, or Individualized Education Programs (Office of Special Education and Rehabilitative Services, 2004). More recently, RTI has been utilized as a model of support for all children. Common principles of RTI include multiple tiers for maximum support for each child, high quality instruction, core curriculum encompassing a research base, a formative and summative data collection system, evidence-based interventions, procedures for identifying selection and revision of instructional practices, and monitoring measures (Jackson et al., 2009).

Both PBS and RTI have significance for culturally considerate school counseling in their multilayered, individualized structures. Both of these models also rely heavily on professional teamwork, giving school counselors opportunities for collegial support, shared responsibility, and greater chance of effecting change schoolwide.

A FEW NEW THOUGHTS ON SOME OLD TECHNIQUES

School counselors and other helping professionals are trained and generally experienced in basic counseling techniques. Active listening skills are important but not always executed with the unconditional positive regard and authenticity children require. Patricia Van Velsor (2004) writes that counselors learn to use "microskills" that help them to act more purposefully with their clients. "These microskills are the threads that the counselor weaves into techniques to help form the intricate tapestry of counseling. . . . Although descriptions of how to apply these skills to counseling with children often include the acknowledgment that children have different cognitive levels and more limited vocabularies than adults, these descriptions often rely heavily on discovering ways to encourage the verbal communication of children" (Van Velsor, 2004, p. 313).

Virginia Axline (1969), noted author of the invaluable *Dibs in Search of Self* and *Play Therapy*, identified eight basic principles of play therapy which are also essential to any counseling intervention with children and most adolescents, although admittedly may not always be practical in terms of time, context, or pressure from other school personnel, administration, or parents. Nonetheless, Axline's principles are an informative basis for work with students and especially for work with student clients whose cultural experience is different from our own:

1. The [counselor] must develop a warm, friend relationship with the child in which a good rapport is established as soon as possible.

2. The [counselor] accepts the child exactly as she or he is.

3. The [counselor] establishes a feeling of permissiveness in the relationship so that the child feels free to express her feelings completely.

4. The [counselor] is alert to recognize the feeling the child is expressing and reflects those feelings back to him in such a manner that he gains insight into his behavior.

5. The [counselor] maintains a deep respect for the child's ability to solve his own problems if given an opportunity to do so. The responsibility to make choices and to institute change is the child's.

6. The [counselor] does not attempt to direct the child's actions or conversation in any manner. The child leads the way; the [counselor] follows.

7. The [counselor] does not attempt to hurry the [counseling]. It is a gradual process and is recognized as such.

8. The [counselor] establishes only those limitations necessary to anchor the counseling to the world of reality and to make the child aware of his or her responsibility. (Axline, 1969, pp. 73–74)

While many children and adolescents tolerate "talk therapy" better than we think, progress is more often made when we meet them on their own playing field. But this is true of any student, client, colleague, or friend. When considering student clients who come from different cultures or who have unique life experiences, our willingness to engage on their terms is the first and most important signal of our capacity to help without bias.

Van Velsor (2004) discusses the difference in reflection when counseling children versus adults. "With adult clients, this translates into reflecting the verbal message communicated. Because children's content may be expressed in actions or play, the counselor working with children must add behavioral tracking to his or her repertoire."

In behavioral tracking, the counselor simply reflects to the child what he or she is doing at any particular time (Van Velsor, 2004). Games and art supplies are staples in most school counseling offices. Having these items and giving them to children to use while in the session does not constitute counseling. Beyond initial introductions, these articles are meant to be a part of the counseling process. To children, they are important extensions of themselves. If we simply leave them to draw random pictures, we run the risk of dismissing the child by dismissing the art.

We must overtly demonstrate we are attending to the child's actions. If we play checkers or Candyland with our student clients and don't learn from how the child responds to the moves she must make, we are missing valuable information. There are also many fine therapeutic games available to counselors, but even these can be easily underutilized or too heavily relied upon to provide easy answers to overworked professionals.

Reflecting meaning and interpreting with child clients likewise revolves more often around play and action rather than verbal communication. In many instances, children catch on to therapy and/or counseling much quicker than their adult counterparts. Children seldom suffer fools gladly. Van Velsor (2004) tells us that the counselor who effectively extracts and imparts meaning in adult communications can do the same with meaning conveyed in a child's communications through play as well as through words and believes there can be a wealth of meaning in children's metaphor. She cites Romig when stating,

> Metaphor is powerful in its capacity to allow the client to confront difficult personal experience while affording an often critical distance from the distressing material. Metaphor may also be central in developmental change processes in counseling, including building relationships and bypassing client resistance, facilitating awareness of emotions and unconscious beliefs, and introducing new perspectives and possibilities. (p. 314)

Concurring with Brems, Van Velsor asserts that whether a counselor interprets meaning to the child and how he or she does so are dependent, in part, on theoretic orientation. Regardless of theoretic inclination, interpretation requires a great degree of rapport in the counselor and student client relationship. This may be particularly important with the child client because children are generally referred to counseling by others (parents or teachers) and may not be seeking insight (Van Velsor, 2004). In other words, *when in doubt, don't.*

Citing Spiegel and Landreth, Van Velsor emphasizes the importance of limit setting in child counseling. Counselors set limits to protect children, materials, themselves, and others. Counselors communicate the boundaries of acceptable behavior, the counselor's interest in keeping the child safe, and interpersonal responsibility (Van Velsor, 2004). In the context of cultural competency, school counselors also can use limit setting to underscore the importance of acceptance, tolerance, and social justice.

Roaten and Schmidt (2009) reiterate that school populations have become much more culturally diverse in recent years and state, " . . . this trend has further contributed to the societal stratification seen in schools, evidenced by the propensity of students to form groups based on socio-economic status, academics, sexual orientation, religion, race/ethnicity, culture and other characteristics." Citing Zimmerman and colleagues in asserting that proactive or remedial interventions that target students' cultural awareness and skills have rarely been fully integrated into schools and counseling programs, Roaten and Schmidt (2009) advocate experiential activities to promote multicultural awareness and respect for diversity. They further state that much of the recent cultural and diversity education curricula emphasize differences and learning about cultures and stress that diversity education should also more effectively promote critical thinking. Experiential activities can be powerful means to stimulate multicultural awareness while assisting students in confronting and overcoming bias (Roaten & Schmidt, 2009).

Roaten and Schmidt (2009) assert experiential learning can be an effective tool, as it (a) encourages students to consider cultural contexts that influence their own behavior, attitudes, and beliefs; (b) engages students in affective learning that assists them in challenging their ethnocentrism and promotes self-awareness; and (c) facilitates students' own cultural experiences in a structured and low-risk environment.

Kim, Green, and Klein (2006) add that instilling multicultural sensitivity through the use of materials such as storybooks is an important part of helping children develop a strong social competence, especially in an increasingly diverse society. Citing numerous studies, they contend multicultural sensitivity enhances social competency which leads to the formation of social networks and particular friendships. Through these friendships, children learn to share, resolve conflict, negotiate, and be more cognitively sophisticated. When able to establish interracial friendships, children demonstrate higher levels of psychosocial maturity.

In addition, there is evidence that experiential activities go beyond cognitive learning and also enhance academic performance by engaging students in affective learning and higher-level thinking skills (Roaten & Schmidt, 2009). Experiential activities require supplies.

Please don't assume I am unaware of budget cuts, cramped office space, or lack of storage options. I am. In addition to struggling with these kinds of stationary challenges, I also spent several years of my professional life on the road doing on-site or in-home therapy. My motto became *have games, will travel*. When I was traveling, I used a very inexpensive rolling suitcase for my supplies. I found a brand new one once at a resale shop for $5.00. Plastic bins are also good storage and can be stored in a closet out of the way if needed.

The following list of items is, in my view, a very basic array of supplies to assist in counseling children and adolescents. There is a short list of things that require some attention to quality; however, most of them are very inexpensive or can be obtained at discounts or by donations. Many of them are likely around your house, waiting for next week's trash collection. My favorite place to shop is the dollar store. Puzzles, stickers, packages of plastic police officers, fire fighters, animals, and other trinkets are always available.

Invest in These Items

- Good pencils—Mirano Black Warrior #2 are my favorite. Keep them sharp.
- 11 × 14 drawing paper. Please don't use copy paper. Good, sturdy drawing paper is worth the cost and signals to the student client that his or her art is important. Your school's art teacher might share some with you.
- Extra large manila envelopes to store the artwork. Use one envelope for each student both for confidentiality reasons and to let the child know you value what she or he has shared.
- Modeling clay—*not play dough.* The odor of clay is less evocative; the clay holds up better and lasts longer and can be reshaped as the child changes.
- Oil pastels for older children who may have more exposure to and control over art media.

Get These Items Wherever You Can

- Crayons—more boxes of fewer colors are best. I recommend the 24 count. Kids love a new box of crayons. Offering buckets of broken and ragged crayons to children is like serving cold coffee to adults.
- Markers
- Multicultural markers
- Good quality construction paper
- Safety scissors—not baby scissors
- Magazines of all kinds for collage
- Bits of wrapping paper, old greeting cards, stickers, fabric swatches
- Basic games like checkers, chess, dominos, and playing cards
- Puzzles no more than 100 pieces so they can be completed during a session
- CD player and several blank CDs so clients can make their own background music or create audio music journals
- Dolls and stuffed animals for comfort and role-play (I don't suggest anatomically correct dolls unless used by trained investigative professionals. These can lead to more confusion than clarity.)
- Several small plastic toys such as soldiers, firefighters, animals, and so on for action play or for behavioral tokens
- Tissues (I'm amazed by how many offices do not have tissues available.)

SOME BRIEF COMMENTS ON BRIEF THERAPIES

There are several models of brief therapy or counseling. Some stem from cognitive-behavioral schools of therapy, some from family systems theory, and others from crisis intervention movements. The establishment of the managed health care industry also had a great deal to do with an increasing trend toward brief models in an effort to control costs of mental health treatment (Wilcoxon, Magnuson, & Norem, 2008). Out of these trends, solution-focused and/or strengths-based counseling have emerged as successful modalities for use in schools.

Solution-focused therapy is grounded on the assumption that for every problem there is a solution. To formulate solutions, the counselor helps the client build on exceptions—times when the problem could have occurred but did not or was less severe (George, 2008). This approach is especially useful for many children as it embraces resiliency and helps build upon strengths. Solution-focused counseling also embraces the child client's worldview, making it a particularly useful modality for working with students from all cultures. Through the use of a "miracle question," the child client's innate propensity for visualization and imagination is utilized to find a clear picture of the solution, even when the problem may not be clearly defined or understood.

Counselors who use solution-focused methods make conscious use of time by engaging the client quickly and keeping him focused on goals and priorities. The counselor works cooperatively with the student client to create solutions built on strengths rather than fixing things or curing illness (Mireau & Inch, 2009).

Critics of solution-focused interventions often assert the approach is simplistic and raise concerns regarding lasting change (J. Linton, 2005). While more longitudinal studies may be needed to validate the efficacy, solution-based counseling has been proven effective in school settings. Anger management, substance abuse, academic achievement, and social skill building are among the issues most commonly addressed by brief counseling techniques. Solution-focused methods have been found useful in enhancing motivation and helping resistant clients (J. Linton, 2005).

Some student clients may not benefit from brief therapy but may be engaged by solution-focused skills in order for school counselors to assess needs and make appropriate referrals. Students who have experienced trauma, have severe emotional disturbance, are actively self-harmful, or are suicidal should be seen for more intensive treatment outside the school setting.

SCHOOL-BASED GROUP COUNSELING

In the timeless text *The Theory and Practice of Group Psychotherapy*, the venerable Irvin Yalom (1985) describes group therapy as "a curious plant in the garden of psychotherapy. It is hardy: the best available research has established that group therapy is effective, as robust as individual therapy. Yet it needs constant tending" (pp. 516–517). Yalom believes group counselors in training profit from (1) observing experienced group therapists at work, (2) close clinical supervision of their early groups, (3) personal group experience, and (4) personal therapeutic work. The following are Yalom's classic elements of group psychotherapy:

1. Installation of Hope
2. Universality
3. Imparting of Information
4. Altruism
5. The Corrective Recapitulation of the Primary Family Group
6. Development of Socializing Techniques
7. Imitative Behavior
8. Interpersonal Learning
9. Group Cohesiveness
10. Catharsis
11. Existential Factors

Although Yalom (1985) practiced from a traditional psychoanalytic/psychodynamic theory base, he concurred with Carl Rogers' assertion that the unconditional positive regard and acceptance among group members was more potent and meaningful than acceptance by the therapist, with the group experience leading to deeper self-exploration, self-understanding, and growth. Group counseling with children and adolescents provides the same opportunities, though the cautions generally applied to counseling and therapies with children need to be heeded.

The ASCA (American School Counselor Association) National Model endorses group work as an important component of comprehensive school counseling programs (American School Counselor Association, 2005). Steen, Bauman, and Smith (2007) cite the ASCA 1999 position statement which reads, " . . . group counseling is an efficient and effective way of dealing with students' developmental problems and situational concerns," and Riva and Haub's 2004 work stating research has consistently supported the effectiveness of group counseling in schools.

School counselors and social workers are notoriously pressed for time. Their multifaceted and widely divergent roles rarely allow for the in-depth or extended individual attention students often need. Frequently, group counseling is the preferred method of service delivery. Conversely, Steen et al. (2007) found that 87% of school counselors polled in a 2006 study indicated that lack of time during the school day was the most common reason groups were not supported and/or conducted in their schools. Other themes that impacted the inclusion of groups in school counseling programs were staff and administration value and support of groups, parent perceptions, and confidentiality issues.

Many factors contribute to the effectiveness of group counseling in schools. Steen et al. (2007) refer to Yalom's element of universality as one—the knowledge that others have similar challenges. Small groups provide a milieu for peer interaction and observation of peer role models. Students not only receive support from others but also have the opportunity to be helpful to others, increasing self-esteem.

Bauer, Sapp, and Johnson (2000) write,

> The school is an ideal location for the use of cognitive-behavioral interventions with students since the underlying assumption of behavior theory is that all behaviors, cognitions, and emotions are learned and, thus, can be modified through instruction. The counseling group is viewed as an educational experience in which group members can learn and practice new behaviors and skills to help them become more successful in school. (p. 42)

Bemak, Chung, and Siroskey-Sabado (2006) assert group counseling is the intervention of choice in schools, citing McClanahan et al.'s 1998 literature review which found group counseling to be better at fostering social competencies, insights, and social skill development. Children facing divorce, students who have poor peer relationships, youth at risk, students challenged by academic success, and multicultural students are among those identified as populations benefitting from group participation.

Leslie Cooley (2009) writes, "We know from research and training that group counseling is the treatment of choice for many adolescents; for this demographic, anything a peer says is far more interesting and influential than anything we could say on our best day" (p. 3). She further writes, "At the elementary level, many of the issues for which students are referred for counseling are social or behavioral in nature. Group counseling is an ideal way to work on the skills necessary to be successful in these areas" (p. 3).

Using the ACSA National Model (American School Counselor Association, 2005) as framework for the development, delivery, and evaluation of the program, Kayer and Sherman (2009) present a successful group model for ninth-grade students to improve academic performance. They focused on three areas:

1. Cognitive and metacognitive skills such as goal setting, time management, and study skills

2. Social skills, including listening and teamwork

3. Self-management skills, including motivation

Steen and colleagues (2007) note three most common types of groups conducted by school counselors in their 2006 study were those dealing with academic skills, anger management, and social skill building but also note that often the anger management groups were court ordered and facilitated by outside counselors.

School-based group counseling programs should serve all students by considering the diverse and individual differences that are valuable to all in a rich multicultural society. The group experience should be relevant and meaningful to the lives of all students. While some topics may promote homogeneity within a group, the more heterogeneous the membership of a group is, the more productive, as there is a better chance to replicate the school culture as a whole. School counselors can encourage diversity in group memberships by reaching out to all segments of the school population. In addition, school counselors must be highly sensitive to how different cultural perceptions and learning styles affect and are influenced by group process (Stroh & Sink, 2002). Multiple studies have shown students from culturally diverse backgrounds have benefited from culturally responsive groups. Data has been presented on the increased self-perception of African American and Portuguese children, the academic improvement, quality of family life and mental health for Mexican American adolescents, the improvement in achievement and interpersonal relationships for Israeli children, and the increased self-esteem and internal locus of control of Native American adolescents (Bemak et al., 2006).

Over the span of my career, I have facilitated many groups in many settings with many populations, including school-age children, but school-based group counseling is not my area of expertise. My experience in treating children, in fact, has led to me doubt the usefulness of group work within school settings. As a respectful researcher, however, I must defer to the practitioners and authors who present evidence to the contrary and to the ASCA National Model. As a transparent reporter, I must also acknowledge those instances in which group work has indeed been effective.

In Chapter 7, I reference a type of group most frequently labeled Gay-Straight Alliances. In these group meetings, students come together to discuss, learn, and become comfortable with differences in sexual orientations/preferences. In my experience, school-based groups have succeeded when they are topic specific, are psycho-educational in process, and function within a set structure which establishes rules of conduct and safety. Steen et al. (2007) found the issue of confidentiality was of concern to many parents, administrators, and students who came from small or rural communities. I have found this to be a large issue in urban schools as well. Each school or school building is its own small community and as quoted in the aforementioned article, "Everyone knows everything about everyone."

To ameliorate concerns about confidentiality and to diffuse the intensity of some group process outcomes which can threaten student functioning within the school environment (and as an art therapist), I advocate for experiential groups. When the focus is on an activity or creative outcome, change can happen as effectively but without the risk of undue self-disclosure or fear of exposure.

ALTERNATIVE MODALITIES AND ADJUNCT THERAPIES

Clinical work with children has always incorporated experiential activities and intertwined talk, art, and play. Children are naturally drawn to the healing qualities of creativity, spontaneous expression, fantasy, and safe communication (Malchiodi, 1999). Creative or expressive therapies are spontaneous and self-generated, self-expressive, and practiced by children according to age, intelligence, maturity, stress, and life experience (Betensky, 1973).

Storytelling, art, free play, and movement are good activities for younger children. Music, art, photography, dance, journaling, writing, and psychodrama appeal to middle and high school age students. Children of all ages with moderate to severe behavior problems often respond well to behavior charts, tangible reinforcement of positive behaviors that are based on attaining new levels of choice, autonomy, or privileges.

When introducing alternative, experiential, expressive, or creative methods to student clients, it is important school counselors have at least some cursory training in how to implement these activities and the materials associated with them. Offering crayons does not make us art therapists; playing music during a session does not make us music or dance therapists. However, neither should crayons nor music be the proprietary vehicles of specialized therapists only. These media have existed and been instinctively used as healing tools for much longer than any specialty.

There is great advantage to supplementing our verbal counseling skills with nonverbal, kinesthetic ones, yet we must also be prudent and thoughtful in choosing those with which we are comfortable, knowledgeable, and which are appropriate to the student client. I was a licensed clinical social worker/psychotherapist for nearly 18 years before I was a board certified art therapist. Prior to being trained as an expressive arts psychotherapist, I used art to facilitate client work, but there were distinct differences in how I made use of art then and how I do so now. In my estimation, the most important difference is that the introduction of art was usually initiated by the client. My clients' intrinsic need to make art and share it with me was, in large part, why I became interested and committed to better understanding the powerful process of art-making as a therapeutic pathway. Another important difference is my role as clinician. Prior to my expressive arts training, I could observe, appreciate, and validate the art brought to and made in my office. Now, I consider myself a grateful guide and honored witness.

Expressive and experiential modalities make the most of sensory and motor function and are naturally acclimated to use with children and adolescents. Movement, vision, touch, sound, and even taste can be incorporated into opportunities for understanding, growth, and change.

Art therapy is based on the belief that the creative process involved in the making of art is healing and life enhancing (American Art Therapy Association, 2010). Art therapists fall into two general categories: the first involves a belief in the inherent healing power of the creative process; the second emphasizes the product as means of symbolic communication (Malchiodi, 1998). Regardless, it is the media which opens the doorway (Simpkinson & Simpkinson, 1998) and therefore is an innate entryway into a child's world. Art can also open a "window of opportunity" (K. Anderson, 2001–2010) by which child clients can view the world of others more clearly.

Music therapy has been defined as a "systemic process of intervention where . . . the client achieves health using musical experiences and relationships that develop through them as dynamic forces of change" (Bonny, 1997). Joseph Moreno (2000), a prominent figure in the field of music therapy, asserts that music therapy is a modern discipline that has many worldwide sources and connections. Many parallels can be seen between modern music therapy and the healing role of music in traditional cultures.

Poetry therapy and bibliotherapy are terms used sometimes synonymously to describe the intentional use of poetry and other forms of literature for healing and personal growth. Written or read material serves as a catalyst for feeling response and discussion. The process entails four essential stages: recognition, examination, juxtaposition (contrasts and comparisons), and application. Goals are to develop accuracy and understanding in perceiving self and others; develop creativity, self-expression, and self-esteem; strengthen interpersonal and communicative skills; vent emotions and release tension; find new meaning through new ideas, insights, and information; and promote change and increase coping skills and adaptive functions (Diaz De Chumaceiro, 1996; Johnson, 1998). These elements are also described relative to use of storybooks to instill multicultural sensitivity.

> Through encountering problems in stories, children are able to project their own struggles onto characters, thereby gaining insight and direction. . . . In the school setting, bibliotherapy has been used with children who experience a wide range of problems such as bereavement, depression, substance use, and behavioral problems. . . . In general, books can provide information and insight, facilitate learning and problem solving, communicated values, and build relationships. . . . More specifically, as they relate to multicultural sensitivity, books can be used to help children develop a sense of identity, an awareness of the ways in which they are different

from others, knowledge about their own and other cultures, and skills to relate effectively with people of different cultural backgrounds. (Kim et al., 2006, pp. 224–226)

Drama therapy helps to tell a story in order to solve a problem, achieve a catharsis, extend depth of experience, understand the meaning of images, and strengthen the ability to observe personal roles while increasing flexibility between roles. A background in theater arts including improvisation, puppetry, role-playing, pantomime, and theater production is optimal. Through drama, student clients may reduce isolation, develop new coping skills and patterns, broaden affect (emotional expression), improve social skills, and develop relationships.

Drama therapy differs from psychodrama, which has roots in spontaneous dramatization but concentrates upon one person's conflict(s). Using action methods, sociometry, role training, and group dynamics, psychodrama facilitates constructive change by simulating life circumstances in order to produce insight and opportunity for clients to practice new skills. Through re-creation and enactment, participants focus upon specific situations in the life of a particular client. Other members of the group, *auxiliaries,* support the *protagonist* by taking on the role of significant others. The counselor then acts as *director,* creating scenes or scenarios to facilitate change. The remaining group members become the *audience.* Psychodrama, when practiced judiciously, can be a dynamic tool for defusing school tensions between individuals and/or groups. School violence and bullying, racial/ethnic tension, and social isolation are all potential subjects which can benefit from a professional skilled in psychodrama techniques (Blatner, 1973).

Movement therapies are based on the assumption that mind and body are interrelated and are defined as "psychotherapeutic use of movement as a process which furthers the emotional, cognitive and physical integration of the individual" (American Dance Therapy Association, 2010). Originally developed because some psychiatric patients were considered too disturbed for traditional treatment, dance therapy gave birth to movement therapies for chronic medical conditions and later for health promotion and disease prevention. Movement modalities are particularly useful with student clients who have been diagnosed with conditions along the autism spectrum or with attention deficit/hyperactivity disorders. Physically challenged students may also benefit from modified movement modalities.

Combining modalities can produce extraordinary results. Art-making to music, dance in response to another student's drum beat, or producing lyric from poetry not only facilitate individual creativity but also stimulate psychic multitasking, problem solving, and conflict resolution skills.

Some additional modalities to consider are sandplay therapy, animal assisted therapy, and outdoor and/or adventure therapy. All of these have merit, but proper training and supervision before practicing any cannot be stressed enough.

ALTERNATIVE MODALITIES IN SUPERVISION

In Chapter 12, I confess my bias that all clinicians need to be clients at some point in their life. I discuss this in the context of self-care for the caregiver, a topic I have studied and about which I have facilitated many workshops. Similarly, supervision is something I not only advocate but also strongly encourage for clinicians at all levels of experience. As I reiterate in Chapter 12, often the personal and professional meet; sometimes, they collide. Supervision ideally helps us to avoid injury to self or others.

For those of us who are seasoned professionals—okay, older than dirt—finding a supervisor who can truly teach us something and confront our clinical blind spots can be difficult. In these instances, finding an alternative form of supervision can be a superb solution.

During a very challenging time in my private practice, I sought the supervision of an art therapist in order to help with countertransferential material I could not otherwise seem to master. Using imagery rather than words, anger, fear, and exhaustion surfaced in living (and dying) color. I found I could purge on paper what I carried from my caseload. Images spoke far more eloquently than words. Through this purging, I felt an immediate release and relief, and I also began to develop a new and very deep appreciation for expressive methods. I explored several. I trained with Michael Harner and Sandra Ingerman and incorporated drumming and journey work into my self-care and spiritual practice. I hesitantly, but courageously, explored authentic movement through a supervision group with Caroline Heckman, a gifted therapist and remarkable teacher, and discovered I could not disconnect my physical body from my body of clinical work.

Expressive, experiential, and creative arts modalities (1) allow cognitively impaired and nonverbal clients to communicate more effectively, (2) encourage access to affect more readily, and (3) establish bonding and therapeutic alliance more quickly. Dallett (1982) points out, however, that expression is not enough. The real synthesis of material comes through putting information and insights gleaned from the expression to work in daily life. This is true for our student clients. This is true for us as professionals.

CHAPTER SUMMARY

Shaun McNiff (2009) is a prolific writer and educator in the field of art therapy. He has worked extensively with cross-cultural groups and finds that the strongest work occurs in the most divergent groups. McNiff writes,

My historical and anthropological investigations have suggested that there is an "eternal recurrence" (Nietzsche) . . . which include the principle of correspondence, creative transformation, symbolic and ceremonial focus, rhythm, catharsis, purposeful action, contagious energy, emergence of personal form, group validation opening to others and giving. . . . The absence of verbal language can actually have positive results, focusing even more energy on the significance of the art object. Body movement, facial expression, and the tone of voice are similarly influenced when there is not a shared verbal language. Other forms of communication by necessity begin to compensate for the loss. (pp. 104–105)

Clients have been referred for nonverbal therapy because of inabilities to communicate through spoken word. By definition, these therapies lend themselves to cross-cultural practice, providing the beginnings of a universal language (McNiff, 2009).

12

Self-Care for the Caregiver

Helping without bias begins with knowing how and why our personal biases came to be and where and when our professional obligations mandate the elimination of them. No one claims this is easy or for the faint of heart. Although it is commonly recognized, both anecdotally and by data, the majority of individuals who choose a helping profession do so, in part, as a response to a need for help at sometime in their lives. Most counselors, clinical social workers, psychotherapists, and psychologists plan to examine the psyches of others rather than scrutinize their own thoughts, motivations, and behaviors.

Some clinical programs require students to experience counseling or psychotherapy during their training. Others strongly urge it but are concerned with legalities of making it a condition of graduation or certification. Far too often, counseling students have no exposure to the "far side of the couch." Neither they nor their clients are served well by this omission. Personal insight and professional development go hand in hand, and there are no two areas where this is more important than when counseling children or in working with culturally diverse populations.

Knowing how strongly I feel about personal awareness and professional accountability, friends and colleagues have asked why I am waiting until the last portion of this book to tell my own story. I do so for a number of reasons.

One of my many road-weary maxims is this: *When in doubt, don't.* There are countless circumstances where this applies, but I often use it when supervising clinicians regarding self-disclosure. Self-disclosure is discussed intermittently throughout the book, but in this instance, I hope to model its use. For many counselors, self-disclosure is an all or nothing proposition. Erring on the side of caution is best. In supervision and sometimes in sessions with clients, I will use another well-worn "Kimism": *If the counselor is more present than the client, the work is out of balance.*

Self-disclosure has a specific place and a steady pace. In reading this book, you already know, assume, or intuit some things about me. If I have done my job, those things have revealed enough to keep you interested but not enough to get in the way. However, as we approach the "physician heal thyself" territory, you may want to know that I've traveled this terrain myself because (1) hypocrisy should be the eighth deadly sin, and (2) it is always good to know someone else has made it through the primordial forest of soul searching and lived to tell the tale.

FULL CIRCLE: MY STORY

My friend and colleague, Bonnie Davis, graciously asked that I contribute to her book, *The Biracial and Multiracial Student Experience: A Journey to Racial Literacy* (2009). My narrative in Chapter 6 primarily presents a professional perspective of biracial and multiracial students from outside the classroom. I also share a bit about my personal understanding of what it is like to be seen as "other."

> I am a very white woman with very noticeable facial scars. It is not uncommon for my child clients to accept me as part of their culture, whatever that may be. If pressed for a definition, they will often decide that I am biracial. I am not, but I am honored by this adoption into their extended, blended families; it is a testament to their unobstructed vision and an instinctive recognition of the color wheel within our internal and external work. (p. 78)

I was not always this self-actualized. If I could insert a sardonic smiley face here, I would. Contrary to popular belief and clinical conjecture, self-actualization is an ongoing, circular, and cyclical experience. We are born, things happen, we are abandoned or nurtured, we learn from it, we change as a result; other things happen, we are stronger so abandonment doesn't wound us so deeply, and we no longer crave to be nurtured; we learn, we change, we wait for the next thing to happen. To some, this may sound dismal and defeatist. If so, it presumes the things that happen are always bad. It does not take into account that good things change us as well.

I was born in southwestern Missouri during a snow storm. Six weeks after I was born, I stopped breathing. An emergency tracheotomy, hundreds of tests, dozens of doctors, and several surgeries later, the congenital hemangioma was contained and eventually removed by a series of experimental procedures which were documented in medical journals and textbooks. I had not been expected to live, so aesthetics were not the surgeons' main priority, and reconstructive surgery in the 1950s was not advanced enough to replace the nerve or muscle damage done during the life-saving operations. Today, the course of treatment for children diagnosed with congenital hemangioma is quite different, and the lasting results far less pronounced.

My family of origin had the ordinary dysfunctions of many American families of the era, but it was mighty in efforts to keep me alive and, accomplishing that, to give me a "normal" life. I had scars, but no one talked about them. As a result, I didn't talk about them but instead got on with my life as if there was nothing different about me. This was particularly interesting given the fact my family moved frequently with my father's career as a hydro-electrical engineer. I perpetually changed schools, met new people, and adapted to new environments.

For many years, I was taken aback if anyone drew attention to my scars or my speech. When they did, it was usually in the form of a blunt quzestion. *What happened to you?* or *What's wrong with you?* These questions stymied me as nothing had happened to me as far as I knew and whatever had been wrong was fixed. I had been assured by my parents I was fine now.

In presentations, I sometimes tell a story about my first clinical "intervention." I was in the third grade and in the lunchroom. In a tone kids would call snarky today, a new classmate asked, "What's wrong with you?" Frustrated, I blurted back, *"Nothing. What's wrong with you?"* The child who had initiated the inquiry looked horrified, began to cry, and then wailed, *"How did you know?!"* I tell this story to illustrate that many children feel there is something wrong with them. I also tell this story to illustrate that difference is equated to "wrong." I learned this very early in life. Subliminally at first, then very deliberately, it became central to my professional development and my career path.

It was not my intention to become a clinical social worker. My bachelor's degree was in writing for mass media, photography, and graphic arts. I was on my way to a graduate degree in writing when I took an unexpected detour. My compromise was to design an independent curriculum in mass media for social services. Along the way, I took a few clinical classes, and as we say in the Ozarks, it was all over but the shoutin.'

Only now in my 50s, does my work history match my age. For most of my clinical life, I have been in private practice or under per diem contract. I am well aware this has been a choice made due to need for control over my own destiny. I have worked with children and adolescents, adults, families, couples, and groups in a variety of settings and locations. I have been a trainer, supervisor, and consultant to schools, public and private agencies, hospitals, and individual practitioners. I have been an educator in many undergraduate and graduate programs in counseling, social work, and art therapy.

For over 20 years, the majority of my clinical practice was working with survivors of sexual trauma. Eventually, my daily calendar became filled with the most severe and complex cases. I was good at my work, but it took a toll. In 2001, I closed my private practice and took some time to complete a postgraduate certification in art psychotherapy. It was one of the best things I have ever done for myself.

My thesis was titled *Full Circle: Countertransference Containment Through Mandala-Making (A Case Study of Closure)*, and in it I wrote, "Recognizing that countertransference is a part of every therapeutic relationship, thorough clinical work is predicated on therapist self-awareness and requires attunement and analysis." Citing Pearlman and Saatvitne (1995), I defined countertransference as, "any response the (counselor) has to his or her client, positive or negative, conscious or unconscious, spoken or unspoken" (2002, p 14).

Simply stated, bias, bigotry, chauvinism, and intolerance is negative countertransference, and we are obliged to examine how it impairs us, how it impacts our clients, and how we may learn to limit its effect on our work. Conversely, we also are privileged by the discovery of how our positive countertransference informs our successes and moves clients beyond their self-imposed limitations.

In *The Biracial and Multiracial Student Experience: A Journey to Racial Literacy* (Davis, 2009) I wrote,

> I think about my own journey of self-discovery and awareness. I began, rather ignorantly as a white woman whose only claim to diversity was that of gender bias. Joining clients in their travels during the years, I have come to realize that my aesthetic challenges—my obvious facial scars—give me early entrée to cultural acceptance. I, too, am seen as different—sometimes less than, sometimes as more than I should be, sometimes as "uppity" for daring to be in the Real World, Re-Creating my life day by day. (p. 84)

SELF-ASSESSMENT TOOLS

There are many models of cultural competence from many different sources and disciplines. In all helping professions, self-awareness is the foundation for multicultural awareness and cultural competency (Saleebey, 1994). Bennett (1993) suggests a model whereby cultural competence moves from *ethnocentric* stages of denial, defense, and minimization, to *ethno-relative* stages of acceptance, adaptation, and integration. Ponterotto, Utsey, and Pedersen (2006) offer the Multicultural Counseling Knowledge and Aware Scale. The prolific Derald W. Sue and David Sue (2008) introduced us to a Multidimensional Model of Cultural Competence which continues to be a classic contribution to the profession.

Sharing a personal and professional interest in cultural equity and racial literacy, Bonnie Davis and I have examined our personal passages and professional paths toward cultural competency in an effort to train others in our respective fields. In 2008, we scoured the literature in search of the perfect professional development model. We found several, such as those I cite previously, but decided no one model suited our multiple purposes so we created an eight-stage Model of Diversity Development.

These eight stages—Acknowledgment of Bias, Assessment of Current Competency, Acceptance of Limitations, Cognitive Restructuring, Expanding Knowledge Base, Skill Building, (Active) Helping Without Bias, and Reparation—are all important steps in attaining cultural consideration and helping without bias. While numerous authors include versions of these measurements, few underscore the necessity of reparation. It isn't enough to verbalize awareness or even to behave without bias. To truly honor the experience of others, it is imperative humility be a part of our practice. To honor the humanness beneath our professional demeanor, we must also recognize we never stop learning. I reiterate: contrary to popular belief and clinical conjecture, self-actualization is an ongoing, circular, and cyclical experience.

The schema in Figure 12.1 illustrates the cyclical nature of human skill building specific to developing culturally considerate counseling skills.

Figure 12.1 Model of Diversity Development

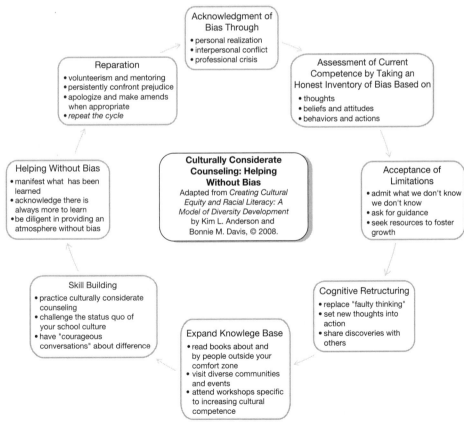

Acknowledgment of bias is the first and most difficult step. Not unlike the 12-step model of recovery, acknowledgment of our addiction to biased beliefs and behaviors can be extremely painful. Awareness and acknowledgment usually doesn't happen on its own. No miracle occurs, no nighttime apparition haunts us into revelation, but usually something does happen to force us to face our deficits. This something often falls into one of three categories: Personal Realization, Interpersonal Conflicts, and/or Professional Crisis.

Personal realization may be silent but is always profound. Examples of personal realization include a family member's marriage to someone from another country, the birth of a biracial or multiracial grandchild, or discovering that a respected colleague is Muslim. Interpersonal conflicts may arise from any of these examples, or they may arise at work between coworkers and escalate to a professional crisis. Name-calling, exclusion based upon race or culture, or refusal to confer with, work with, or hire persons of color, sexual orientation, or ability can result in sanctions, administrative leave, or even dismissal.

Assessment of current aptitude is necessary to determine what has been driving our biases. There are many indexes and scales to determine prejudice and cultural competency, and we can never have too many tools, though no source is more important than our own heart and mind. As helpers, we came to this work knowing how to size up situations and short comings. Yes, it is more difficult to dispassionately assess ourselves, yet passion is what bias is all about: passionate positions taken for or against a person simply by virtue of their position within a specific group.

Assessment must include our *thoughts, beliefs,* and *attitudes* and our *behaviors* and *actions.* What do we think about others? What do we think about specific groups of people? Our thoughts are comprised of information—that which we know about something, either through experience or research. The information we have may be accurate, or it may incomplete. It may have come to us from misguided or unscrupulous sources. Thoughts may propel our beliefs and attitudes; thoughts alone do not create them.

Beliefs are rarely proven to be true but arrived at over time. Information, experience, and our own culture reinforce our beliefs. Because beliefs are difficult to prove, they are also difficult to disprove. Challenging beliefs sometimes leads to war. America is a country built on beliefs passed off as truths. It is a part of our Constitution: *We hold these truths to be self-evident.* They had a brilliant idea and executed it well, but let's not forget that the vast majority of the men who forged that document also owned slaves.

Attitudes are thoughts and beliefs manifested in how we approach people, ideas, and change. Our attitudes are conveyed through words, affect, mannerisms, carriage, dress, and environment. Words may be powerful, but these other expressions can announce attitudes at even higher volumes.

Acceptance of limitations is humbling. We are forced to admit *what we don't know we don't know.* My friend Bonnie Davis stresses the importance of this in her books and in her presentations. Bonnie urges us to accept that this enhances our competency and clears our cultural lens (Davis, 2006). We ask our student clients to be open to learning new ways of thinking about old habits. We too must be open to recognizing our own limits. I try to be particularly aware of this as a specialist in diversity issues. Asking for guidance is difficult for those of us who do training on these topics, but it is essential. There is always someone who knows more, and more important, there are always people within culturally diverse communities willing to educate in an effort to eliminate stereotypes and prejudice. Seeking resources to foster growth includes finding these individuals, attending workshops, and reading both mainstream and academic articles and books to increase awareness and enhance our knowledge base.

I readily admit a bias of my own. In training presentations, I think I can always spot the overworked school counselor or social worker who is exhausted by attendance of one more workshop on multiculturalism. The sullen face, the slow amble into the room, the bulging tote bag, the armload of books, and the deep sigh as she sits down in the last row of chairs signal "retirement," "cynical," "burn-out." Instead of trying to make the presentation I'm about to give helpful and invigorating for her, I dismiss her and focus on the excited, bright-eyed novice on the second row aisle seat who volunteers for all my activities. My limitation here is that I think I know this woman because I know her exhaustion, her burn-out, and her seen-it-all attitude. What I don't know is she has just gotten off the phone with her husband about a problem with her own child, or that she has been caring for her aging parent who has Alzheimer's, or that she herself has been recently diagnosed with stage two ovarian cancer and has been receiving chemotherapy for the past month. What I don't know doesn't help her.

Cognitive restructuring is a term used in behavioral therapies but is applicable to many situations. Cognitive restructuring replaces "faulty thinking" with thoughts derived from accurate information and fundamental understanding of the issue or situation at hand. While this is important, it is relatively useless unless these new thoughts are put into action by behaving differently. For example, my mother grew up thinking, "Gay people were weird and shouldn't be trusted." Years later, after getting to know a friend of mine, she would send birthday cards and Christmas presents. When Mom came to visit me, she would always ask if we were going to visit Debbie. My mother didn't invite very many "outsiders" in, but she came to know that Debbie was kind and funny, and most important, Deb was respectful and cooked a really good meal.

Mom shared this discovery with others on a limited basis, but she did become far more vocal about hate crimes, gay jokes, and slurs when she heard them at work or from other family members.

Expanding knowledge base comes second nature to educators when it involves hard science, teaching strategies, or pedagogy. To become culturally competent, we need to *experience* cultures different from our own, not just acknowledge the existence of them. Reading books about and by people outside your comfort zone is a good way to get started. Learn from a distance at first, then acquaint yourself firsthand by visiting diverse communities and events. Even if you are frustrated by professional mandates, attend workshops specific to increasing cultural competence. Look for training conducted by professionals unknown to you, those given by culturally diverse presenters or experiential workshops which integrate creative process with didactic content.

Skill building involves the practice of culturally considerate counseling. Put new understanding to work by implementing strategies found within this and other texts or workshops. Challenge the status quo of your school culture. Become an identified advocate of cultural consideration and a monitor of the ASCA (American School Counselor Association) National Model at your school. Have "courageous conversations" about difference (Singleton & Linton, 2006). Whether one on one or in faculty and administrative meetings, lead the discussion of multiculturalism and diversity.

Active helping without bias requires manifesting what you have learned. Cultural consideration is useless without demonstrative action. Students, families, colleagues, administration, and community must be able to identify our capabilities as counselors who are open to all students and strive to help without bias. To truly be competent in any thing we do, we must acknowledge there is always more to learn. My friend Bonnie writes, "Knowing what I don't know I don't know continues to expand rather than diminish my life" (Davis, 2006, p. 45). Be diligent in providing an atmosphere without bias. Use journaling, calendars, and student monitors to help keep track of successes and blunders. Remember you will have both.

Reparation is seldom seen in models of cultural competency. My hypothesis is that many academic researchers and counselor educators are focused on other aspects of creating competency within their respective professions. Although the social justice movement has been alive and well for several decades, mention of it as a foundation of cultural competence in the school counseling context has only recently been noted. Reparation is a large component of social justice and can be accomplished in a variety of ways. Volunteerism and mentoring can be viewed as a societal "give back," returning or restoring time and respect to a neighborhood but should always be done in deference to elders or leaders in the community. Ask, "What can I do?" Never say, "Let me tell you what needs to be done." Persistently confront prejudice. This models appropriate attitudes and behaviors and should happen in the classroom, the hallways, sometimes even in school board meetings. Apologize and make amends when and where appropriate. While it won't make a thoughtless assumption, remark, or behavior go away, verbally acknowledging our insensitivity and incompetence does temper the situation and opens the door to repairing relationships.

Repeat the cycle; start from the beginning. We may evolve, but we are never finished. Humility is never far from humanity in the dictionary or in life. If not nudged to do so by realization, conflict, or crisis, acknowledgment and subsequent assessment of bias should be placed literally and figuratively on our competency calendar. Choose a time period intrinsic to your personal wisdom clock and mark "Cultural Sensitivity Upgrade" on your primary calendar. Consider this your annual worldview checkup. Eventually, it will become a part of your personal and professional identity.

WHERE PERSONAL AND PROFESSIONAL DEVELOPMENT MEET

Our professional plotlines begin in our personal narratives. We can glean glimpses of our professional identity formation in childhood games, imaginary friends, and favorite toys. Adolescent friends, room decor, music, and extracurricular activities can tell part of the story. Our first job, favorite college professor, first true love and how it ended can shape how we enter and exit relationships with clients and colleagues. The adult professional we become leads to proficiencies and policy positions. In midlife, we begin to integrate that which we hold dear, and we start to let go of cumbersome clutter. Moving into elder space, we take stock, hold steady, share wisdom, breathe deeply.

I had two favorite play activities: Lone Woman on the Prairie and teacher. Lone Woman on the Prairie involved making a buckboard out of my desk and a bed full of abandoned stuffed animals and multitonal dolls I had rescued from various tragedies. I was usually besieged by local Indians, then befriended. My wagonload of foster children and I were adopted by the tribe and lived happily ever after.

When I played teacher, I was far more interested in setting up the room and acquiring the proper office products. I would scavenge paper, pens, and notebooks where ever I could find them. Today, I am still in search of the perfect writing utensil.

Consider the toys and games you enjoyed as a child, the music you played as a teenager, your favorite movie. What themes carry through your life? They may tell you a great deal about what themes you carry into your work as a helping professional.

WHEN THE PERSONAL AND PROFESSIONAL COLLIDE

Personal narratives are often fraught with writer's block; professional plotlines may take unexpected twists. Individual, occupational, and global circumstances all impact our ability or inability to help effectively. These circumstances influence our private lives, influence the way in which we do our public jobs, and may result in outcomes we did not anticipate.

Many studies report school counselors are at risk for professional burnout as a result of their wide variety of service-oriented roles. Role conflict and role ambiguity are two specific occupational stressors that school counselors experience. Effective balance of various professional and personal roles factors in job satisfaction, life satisfaction, and general well-being (Bryant & Constantine, 2006).

Individual circumstances involving situations such as illness, family matters, or a death are profound, and spillage into our work is inevitable. Occupational circumstances such as changes in job or school policies, conflicts within the work environment, or the challenge of dual relationships naturally affect our work performance. Global circumstances (significant historic or political events, natural disasters, war) may intrude upon our professional space without time to prepare.

Health is a personal issue, but when illness causes visible symptoms, causes absenteeism, or affects work performance, we must recognize our limitations and adjust for them. Family matters are equally personal. Problems with personal relationships, children, aging parents, or issues such as a spouse's job loss or military deployment ride with us to work each day. Certainly, supervisors, administrators, and some coworkers need to be apprised of situations that may require attention during ordinary work days or a temporary leave of absence, but finding a truthful, yet boundaried and balanced way of sharing personal information is important to privacy and comfort levels.

One of the least researched and documented clinical topics is that of how death affects members of the helping professions. Bereavement time is usually allotted for the death of a family member, but support seldom extends beyond the immediate loss or for those deaths that are not considered "family." The death of a close friend or colleague, the death of a beloved pet, or even the death of a student or client are all significant but rarely acknowledged. Consequently, counselors resort to burying their feelings about loss and return before they may be truly ready to resume their work.

Occupational circumstances may be dealt with overtly in staff meetings or professional development venues, yet the emotional consequences of changes in administration, job descriptions, budget crises, conflicts with colleagues, or disciplinary actions follow professionals into the hallways and the counseling office. In each instance, it is imperative the school counselor be conscious and conscientious about boundaries and does his or her best to separate feelings about the work environment from work with students and their families.

Boundary issues occur when professionals face conflicts of interest in the form of *dual relationships* (Reamer, 2003) and are nearly inevitable for school counselors and present an enormous challenge for professionals of every skill level. A dual relationship is created whenever the role of counselor is combined with another relationship (Moleski & Kiselica, 2005). A professional enters into a dual relationship when he or she assumes a second role with a client but cannot always be avoided (Reamer, 2003). This is especially true in small or rural communities and within a school setting. Dual relationships can come about in two ways: by choice and by chance. When formed as a result of a conscious choice made by the counselor, the potential consequences must be examined. In some instances, school counselors have little choice about engaging in a dual relationship such as when their own children attend the same school, they are involved in community organizations with parents of students they counsel, or chance encounters with students and their families at doctor's offices or grocery stores. In working with student clients from other cultures, counselors often find themselves crossing boundaries to promote the counseling relationship. Receptiveness to a student client's culture sometimes leads us to cross into additional relationships in order to further the helping relationship (Moleski & Kiselica, 2005).

To manage these issues effectively, one must develop a clear understanding of what distinguishes unethical (harmful) relationships from ethical (acceptable) ones. A dual relationship is unethical and/or harmful when it is likely to interfere with professional discretion; interfere with professional judgment; exploit student clients, colleagues, or others to further the professional's personal interest; and harm student clients, colleagues, or third parties (Reamer, 2003).

Global circumstances seem to reach into our lives and into our schools at unprecedented rates these days. Some inspire hope and change; others arouse fear and anguish. In the fall 2007 issue of *Journal of Humanistic Counseling, Education, and Development,* Norma L. Day-Vines wrote, "It is ironic that I would sit down to prepare a manuscript about wellness during the midst of the horrendous loss of 33 Virginia Tech students and faculty on Monday, April 16, 2007, as I grapple with personal feelings of dread, confusion, and sadness" (p. 242). She goes on to write,

> I feel a certain queasiness as I come to the inevitable realization that this incident could have occurred on any campus, including mine, that the frequency with which arbitrary and capricious acts of violence have occurred with the recent past (e.g., Columbine High School, 9/11, the sniper attacks) have undermined our collective sense of safety and security, and to add to this conundrum,

conventional forms of power and privilege seem to no longer provide a protective aegis for society. (Day-Vines, 2007, p. 242)

Day-Vines words both validate and haunt me on this day as I write
these pages a few short days after the massive earthquake in Haiti. Images
of rubble and ruin have run on every network and cable channel, a country of vibrant colors now monotone beneath the pallid dust of destruction
and despair. Perhaps, too, like Dr. Day-Vines, I am appalled at oppor-
tunistic commentators whose words are as much of an aftershock as the
actual ones in Port au Prince: *Haiti made a deal with the devil? The people of
Haiti deserve this because they rose against slavery? The current administration
will use this to pander to people of color?*

What do we do with our own feelings when our student clients need
comfort and reassurance they will not be swallowed whole by the earth
or defamed by verbiage of an "unintended consequence of the First
Amendment" (Maddow, 2010). What do we say to our Haitian students
who are worried about relatives they cannot reach by phone when we are
despondent because our own family members are missionaries and we
haven't heard from them either?

Norma Day-Vines says,

We have no recourse but to mine our reservoirs of wellness, even
in the midst of tragedy. The seemingly impossible juxtaposition
of two diametrically opposed states (wellness midst tragedy and
adversity), will likely lead the journey toward healing and wholeness. It is in this vein that I try to identify my personal efforts to
maintain wellness. . . . (2007, p. 242)

Self-care is fundamental to caring for others. Those of us in the
position of influencing the lives of others—especially the delicate lives
of children—are obligated to pursue our own wellness. Day-Vines and
Holcomb-McCoy (2007) cite Myers when defining wellness as the "maxi-
mizing of human potential through positive life-style choices" and Ardell
when stating that "wellness is a conscious and intentional approach to an
advanced state of physical and psychological and/or spiritual health."
They further cite Greenberg who offered a definition of wellness that "integrates social, mental, emotional, spiritual, and physical components."

Day-Vines and Holcomb-McCoy (2007) note that despite the growing
emphasis on wellness and models of wellness in the counseling literature,
the examination of wellness among counselors has received little attention. "Even more surprising is the omission of a discussion regarding
the cultural implications of counselors' wellness" (p. 83). Day-Vines and
Holcomb-McCoy (2007) concur with other authors when stating that
mental health professionals cannot separate wellness from issues of social
justice and write,

At the personal level, people need to be able to exercise control over their lives in a manner that leads to personal empowerment. Relational needs involve a concern for humanity and respect for diversity. Collective needs are focused on economic well-being, safety, and security, which are embodied within the principles of social justice, equality, and structural change. (p. 83)

Bryant and Constantine (2006) write, "Counselor wellness can be considered along social, emotional, cognitive, spiritual and vocational domains. Counselors . . . profit from cultivating personal and career care plans that systematically and comprehensively address these six life areas and the roles and role conflicts within these areas." They assert that role conflict highlighted through values clarification might be resolved in a number of ways including quality clinical supervision, active involvement in state and national associations, and, like Day-Vines and Holcomb-McCoy, Bryant and Constantine are proponents of a commitment to social justice and advocacy to affect lasting personal, professional, and systemic change.

Afterword

What Is a School Without Bias?

Recently, I received an e-mail forward from a colleague. Within the e-mail was a link to forums critical of white people doing "antiracist" work. I receive this while I, a white woman, am finishing a book about eliminating bias within helping professions. I keep writing, but for several days, I am in a quandary. I agree with much of what was written, but I find that on some level, I am also offended, and I am embarrassed—perhaps even a bit ashamed. These writers are scholars, educators, activists, and I admire them and the work they do. I admire the honesty with which they write about the oxymoron of white antiracism. I understand it, agree with it, and support it. But does it mean I should not be writing a book about eliminating bias?

When I received the e-mail (from a white male colleague) suggesting we not respond openly to an open letter because it might offend the writer, I was offended by the implication. I am clear that as a white woman, I have no business telling people of color or different ability how to be activists or how to achieve justice. But to suggest I am misguided out of a misplaced and narcissistic sense of altruism or by profit in sharing what I know as a white counselor treating children and families of all hues and views, feels stifling and biased to me. To suggest that I shouldn't respond for fear of offending a writer whose culture is different from my own feels even worse and even more replicating of societal fear of *others*. Especially when all I want to say is simply, "Tell me more. I want to learn."

My early degrees were focused in mass media and media for social services. I believe helping professions can sometimes be helped by the dispassionate assessment of those outside our field. Mauricio Velásquez is the president of the Diversity Training Group, a professional group which provides diversity training to businesses and corporations. Although educators and counselors ordinarily do not pull from corporate resources,

I am intrigued by Velázquez's material outlining why diversity training fails and why it succeeds. I have adapted and tailored this material for schools. Diversity training fails for the following reasons:

1. The training is coming out of a governing board or office rather than from the organization as a whole. A steering committee must be made up of staff from a representative cross section of the institution.

2. The training is done because it is "right" or "moral" rather than understanding the connection between diversity and the bottom line. In educational terms, this means achievement.

3. Training is all that happens. Nothing happens beyond.

4. The training has the support of administration but not their commitment.

5. The training is "off the shelf" and not custom designed to meet the unique needs of the particular school or district.

6. Training is developed and led solely by outside consultants and trainers who have no ownership of implementation.

7. The training is developed without a formal needs assessment and may not address key barriers within a distinct school or district.

8. The training may be awareness based but provides no practical skills or strategies.

9. No internal resources are identified or developed to "keep the fires burning."

10. There is no formal follow up, ongoing attention, periodic assessment, or reevaluation from either internal or external experts.

Diversity training succeeds when the following are in place:

1. Training is developed through a partnership of internal staff and external experts.

2. There is a designated leader with authority to advocate change. He or she handpicks the best package and presenter for the school or district and participates in the training.

3. Training material is supported by sound research.

4. The school culture is supportive and committed to continuous learning and change.

5. Training is "skill based." Participants come away feeling they have new tools for their kit.

6. Skills can be transferred from the training room to the classroom, staff meetings, and school community.

7. Outcomes do not rely on one person to effect actual change.

8. Change doesn't occur in a vacuum and must be supported by other initiatives and activities. Training alone is not a cure-all but a piece of a progressive puzzle.

9. Training is thoroughly planned, implemented, and measured.

10. Training inspires, promotes action, and creates change which allows for a more inclusive environment for students, families, educators, staff, and administration. (Velasquez, 2009)

Pedrotti, Edwards, and Lopez (2008) write, "School Counselors need multiple resources to assists today's students in developing to their fullest potential. This development might often be measured outwardly by academic success; however, psychological and emotional well-being of students is a large part of this success" (p. 100). The authors go on to define "the construct of hope" as a bidimensional characteristic, consisting of an agency component and a pathways component. Helping school counselors to enhance individual strengths through the promotion of characteristics such as hope may result in multiple benefits for students and their school environments at large" (p. 100).

Pedrotti et al. (2008) cite Snyder and colleagues (2006) when discussing the "Hope Theory." Goals are the anchor of Hope Theory. To reach goals, individuals must perceive they are capable of imagining one or more routes (pathways). Agency or motivation is another component, propelling individuals to initiate and sustain movement toward their goals. Within this Hope Theory, it is important for school counselors to take cultural context into account in developing appropriate interventions for students of all backgrounds. In considering hope as it applies to diverse populations, it is important to be aware of differences in time, value systems, and feasibility of personal choice. Hope has been linked to self-esteem, self-worth, quality of life, and academic achievement and vocational identity (Pedrotti et al., 2008, p. 100).

"School counselors may have a unique vantage point within the school environment to contemplate how to improve hope within students, teachers, staff, and administrators," write Pedrotti et al. (2008). "To this end, changes must often be facilitated at the macro level, and recognition of an overarching goal of health and wellness promotion is valuable from an administration perspective. . . . The development of programs that create an environment that facilitates respect for diversity is another essential area."

School counselors become agents of social justice when creating, implementing, and supporting school-based interventions designed to promote school success. Culturally relevant interventions that target youth from diverse backgrounds are especially important (Howard, Olberg, & Scott, 2006).

The Achieving Success Identity Pathways is a program that incorporates the four main components of the ASCA National Model: theoretical foundation underlying the profession, a management system for the school counseling programs, a service delivery system, and accountability methods. By approaching school counseling from a social justice perspective, culturally diverse youth are acknowledged through creating, implementing, and supporting school-based interventions designed to promote academic success and facilitate positive life transitions (Howard et al., 2006).

Another framework for social justice in schools is that of the Ecological Developmental Cognitive Framework which integrates developmental cognitive theory, developmental contextualism, and ecological systems models (Howard et al., 2006). Challenging the predispositions of bias, this framework is a critical aspect of teaching and empowerment and requires school counselors to believe change is possible regardless of an individual's past or current situation. Daily challenges, these predispositions must be done at the macro, exo, and microsystemic levels.

As cultural mediators with a redefined social justice and advocacy role, school counselors may intervene for culturally diverse students in educational systems and communities to eliminate institutional barriers and cultural biases. Except in a few instances, the focus of school counseling has been on self-awareness first. As school populations shift, counselors will likely be required to develop and maintain between a self and other focus, embedded within systems theory for the purposes of mediating the cultural context of the school and community (Portman, 2009). "Professional identity is complex and best viewed eco-contextually," write R. Lewis and Hatch (2008). Social identities such as race, ethnicity, religion, economic status, social class, gender, nationality, chosen interests, sexual identity, politics, and personal history are embedded within our professional identities, influencing both inner and outer worlds.

Nelson and Bustamante (2009) interpret recent research as indicating that many counselors may need insight regarding ways in which to become educational leaders to consistently improve and impact student achievement. Specifically, this is the new focus of school counseling, which attributes whole school and system concerns and issues. There may be a gap in counselor educators' knowledge and expertise between the traditional school counselor role and the transforming role. For today's school counselors, the leadership path should include the entire school staff. The theoretical framework emphasizes the transformational process of leadership. Education Trust and counseling scholars have challenged the counseling profession to develop new ways for school counselors to serve as leaders in today's educational setting. The new role for school counselors includes a focus on addressing school system factors that influence student development.

School counselor educators are in a position to introduce conversations and advocate social justice, promoting inclusion, more agent status, expanded notions and leadership, and an understanding that all students have islands of competence. "Counselor educators have important roles in assisting preservice school counselors to gain cultural consciousness and the knowledge, attitude, and skills necessary to respectfully enter diverse school communities" (R. Lewis & Hatch, 2008). Counselor educators can "promote conversations on issues such as white privilege, institutional racism, and more. Although difficult, such conversations bring to light that diverse communities are resilient, life enhancing, and open up possibilities for all who are engaged in contributing to them."

Portman (2009) suggests 10 functions for school counselors who are thrust into the role of cultural mediator:

1. Gather and examine school demographic data.

2. Develop an awareness of cultural backgrounds of *all* stakeholders (students, parents, teachers, staff, administrators, and neighboring communities).

3. Communicate with family and community organizations regarding cultural diversity.

4. Seek further education in cultural competence and linguistic skills acquisition.

5. Work and think "outside the box" to affect ongoing social constructions.

6. Facilitate access to helping resources and social service agencies.

7. Help culturally diverse students gain intrapersonal skills to facilitate relationship building.

8. Help culturally diverse students develop social mediation skills to gain knowledge of cultural tools.

9. Create a supportive and encouraging culturally diverse school and community climate.

10. Serve as an information hub for culturally diverse families.

Howard, Olberg, and Scott (2006) explain that when youth understand they have been heard and their difficulties acknowledged, it becomes easier for them to overcome obstacles and write, "By creating educational experiences at school that communicate trust, support, safety, hope, power, control, peace, wholeness, competence, and justice, we can assist youth to rewrite their core beliefs about themselves and the world in which they live."

What is a school without bias? I hope it is not a figment of my imagination. I hope it is an attainable goal for schools in the foreseeable future.

Charles Dickens (1859/1993) opens A *Tale of Two Cities* with

> It was the best of times, it was the worst of times; it was the age of wisdom, it was the age of foolishness; it was the epoch of belief, it was the epoch of incredulity; it was the season of Light, it was the season of Darkness; it was the spring of hope, it was the winter of despair; we had everything before us, we had nothing before us; we were all going directly to Heaven, we were all going the other way. (p. 1)

For all the foolishness and despair in the world today, I know there is hope in change and still believe we have everything before us.

Resources

CHAPTER 1 RESOURCES

American School Counselor Association	www.schoolcounselor.org
Amnesty International	www.amnesty.org
The Equity Alliance	www.equityallianceatasu.org
Human Rights Watch	www.hrw.org
International Institute	www.iistl.org
National Association for Multicultural Education	www.nameorg.org
National Center for Cultural Competence	nccc.georgetown.edu/index.html
Military Family Resources	www.militaryfamily.org www.mfri.purdue.edu/content/ file/HowtoHelp_teacher.pdf www.ed.gov/about/offices/list/ os/homefront/homefront.pdf
Southern Poverty Law Center	www.splcenter.org
Teaching Tolerance	www.tolerance.org
The White Privilege Conference	www.uccs.edu/~wpc

CHAPTER 2 RESOURCES

Anti-Defamation League	www.adl.org
Ontario Consultants on Religious Tolerance	Box 27026 Kingston, ON Canada K7M 8W5 PO Box 128 Watertown, NY 13601-0128 Fax (613) 547-9015 http://www.religioustolerance.org
The PJ Library	www.pjlibrary.org

CHAPTER 3 RESOURCES

Disability Resources	www.disabilityresources.org
Disability Rights, Education, & Defense Fund	www.dredf.org
National Down Syndrome Society	www.ndss.org

CHAPTER 4 RESOURCES

Eating by the Light of the Moon: How Women Can Transform Their Relationships With Food Through Myths, Metaphors, and Storytelling	Author Anita Johnston Gürze Books, 1996
National Eating Disorders Association	www.nationaleatingdisorders.org
Something Fishy	www.something-fishy.org
The Tao of Eating: Feeding Your Soul Through Everyday Experiences With Food	Author Linda R. Harper Innisfree Press, 1993

CHAPTER 5 RESOURCES

Autism Speaks	www.autismspeaks.org
National Autism Association	www.nationalautismassociation.org
National Institutes of Health (NIH)	9000 Rockville Pike Bethesda, MD 20892 www.nih.gov
National Alliance of Mental Illness	3803 N. Fairfax Drive, Suite 100 Arlington, VA 22203 (703) 524-7600 Fax: (703) 524-9094 www.nami.org

CHAPTER 6 RESOURCES

Child Welfare Information Gateway Children's Bureau/ACYF	1250 Maryland Avenue, SW, Eighth Floor Washington, DC 20024 (800) 394-3366 www.childwelfare.gov
The Ophelia Project	www.opheliaproject.org

CHAPTER 7 RESOURCES

American Association of University Women	www.aauw.org
Design Girls: Equity Alliance at ASU	Arizona State University Interdisciplinary B353 PO Box 870211 Tempe, AZ 85287-0211
Digital Sisters	www.digital-sistas.org
The End of Innocence: A Memoir	Authors Chastity Bono and Michele Kort Advocate Books, 2003
Expanding Your Horizons	www.expandingyourhorizons.org
Family Outing: A Guide to the Coming-Out Process for Gays, Lesbians, and Their Families	Authors Chastity Bono and Billie Fitzpatrick Little, Brown, & Company, 1999
Girls Inc.	www.girlsinc.org
GLSEN, the Gay, Lesbian and Straight Education Network	www.glsen.org
LAMBDA	www.lambda.org
National Center for Lesbian Rights	www.nclrights.org
National Abstinence Education Association	www.abstinenceassociation.org
New Moon Magazine	www.newmoon.com
Parents and Friends of Lesbians and Gays	www.pflag.org
Planned Parenthood	www.plannedparenthood.org
Real Boys' Voices	Author William Pollack Random House, 2000
Tough Guise: Violence, Media and Crisis of Masculinity (Video)	Media Education Foundation www.mediaed.org
Why Boys Don't Talk and Why We Care: A Mother's Guide to Connection	Authors Susan Morris Shaffer and Linda Perlman Gordon Mid-Atlantic Equity Consortium, 2000 www.maec.org

Women's Educational Equity Act	www.edc.org/womensequity
Women's Bodies, Women's Wisdom: Creating Physical and Emotional Health and Healing	Author Christiane Northrup, MD Bantom Books, 1995, 2006
Victims No Longer: Men Recovering From Incest and Other Sexual Child Abuse	Author Mike Lew Nevraumont Publishing Company, 1988

CHAPTER 8 RESOURCES

National Network of Partnership Schools	Johns Hopkins University 3003 N. Charles Street, Suite 200 Baltimore, MD 21218 (410) 516-8800 Fax: (410) 516-8890 www.csos.jhu.edu/p2000/center.htm
National Parent Teacher Organizations	541 N Fairbanks Court, Suite 1300 Chicago, IL 60611-3396 (312) 670–6782 Toll-Free: (800) 307-4PTA (4782) Fax: (312) 670-6783 www.pta.org
National Service Learning Partnership	www.service-learningpartnership.org
National Service Resource Center	ETR Associates 4 Carbonero Way Scotts Valley, CA 95066 (800) 860-2684 or (831) 438-4060 TTY: (831) 461-0205 www.nationalserviceresources.org

CHAPTER 9 RESOURCES

American School Counselor Association	www.schoolcounselor.org
Association for Supervision and Curriculum Development	www.ascd.org
National Staff Development Council	www.nsdc.org

CHAPTER 10 RESOURCES

CharacterPlus

1460 Craig Road
St. Louis, MO 63146
(800) 835-8282
Fax: (314) 692-9788
www.characterplus.org

Educating for Change

www.educatingforchange.com

Helping Without Bias

www.helpingwithoutbias.com

CHAPTER 11 RESOURCES

American Art Therapy
Association (AATA)

www.arttherapy.org

American Dance Therapy
Association (ADTA)

www.adta.org

Association for
Experiential Education

www.aee.org

Band Shades:
Multicultural Bandages

www.bandshades.com

Crayola Corporation

www.crayola.com

Diversity Tool Kit

www.diversity.aclin.org

Enchanted Learning

www.enchantedlearning.com

*The Healing Power of Play:
Working With Abused Children*

Author Eliana Gil
Guilford Press, 1991

The Multicultural Toy Box

www.multiculturaltoybox.com

National Art Educators
Association

www.arteducators.org

National Association for
Poetry Therapy

www.poetrytherapy.org

National Association of
Drama Therapy (NADT)

www.nadt.org

Patty Cake Doll Company

www.pattycakedoll.com

CHAPTER 12 RESOURCES

The Artist's Way	Author Julia Cameron Jeremy P. Tarcher/Penguin, 1992
Between Therapists: The Processing of Transference and Countertransference Material	Author Arthur Robbins Jessica Kingsley Publishers, 1988
On Being a Therapist	Author Jeffrey Kottler Jossey-Bass Publishers, 1993
The Soul of Psychotherapy: Recapturing the Spiritual Dimension in the Therapeutic Encounter	Author Carlton Cornett The Free Press, 1998
The Vein of Gold: A Journey to Your Creative Heart	Author Julia Cameron Jeremy P. Tarcher/Penguin, 1997
Walking in This World: The Practical Art of Creativity	Author Julia Cameron Jeremy P. Tarcher/Penguin, 2003

References

Ahmed, S., & Reddy, L. A. (2007). Understanding the mental health needs of American Muslims: Recommendations and considerations for practice. *Journal of Multicultural Counseling and Development, 35*, 207–218.

Amatea, E. S., & West-Olatunji, C. A. (2007). Joining the conversation about educating our poorest children: Emerging leadership roles for school counselors in high-poverty school. *Professional School Counseling, 11*(2).

Ament, J. (2000–2001). *National Jewish population survey.* Jewish Federation of North America. New York: United Jewish Communities.

American Anthropological Association. (1998). *American Anthropological Association statement on "race."* Arlington, VA: American Anthropological Association.

American Art Therapy Association. (2010, January). *American art therapy.* Alexandria, VA: American Art Therapy Association.

American Association of Physical Anthropologists. (1996). AAPA statement on biological aspects of race. *American Journal of Physical Anthropology, 101*, 569–570.

American Dance Therapy Association. (2010). *What is dance therapy?* Retrieved July 9, 2010, from http://www.adta.org/Default.aspx?pageId=378213.

American Psychiatric Association. (2006). *Diagnostic and statistical manual of mental disorders.* Arlington, VA: American Psyciatric Association.

American Psychiatric Association. (1973). *Position statement on homosexuality.* Arlington, VA: American Psyciatric Association.

American Psychological Association. (1998). *Guidelines for psychotherapy with lesbian, gay, and bisexual clients.* Washington, DC: American Psychological Association.

American School Counselor Association. (2007). *The professional school counselor and LGBTQ youth.* Washington, DC: American School Counselor Association.

American School Counselor Association. (2005). *The ASCA National Model: A framework for school counseling programs* (2nd ed.). Alexandria, VA: American School Counselor Association.

American School Counselor Association. (2004, 1999, 1993, 1988). *The professional school counselor and cultural diversity.* Alexandria, VA: American School Counselor Association.

American Speech-Launguage-Hearing Association. (1993). *Definitions of communication disorders and variations.* Rockville, MD: American Speech-Language-Hearing Association.

Anderson, B. (2010). *Purity pledges make sense for teens.* Retrieved January 18, 2010, from Minnosota Family Council: http://www.mfc.org/contents/article.cfm?id=35

Anderson, K. (2002, Summer). *Full circle: Contertransference containment through mandala-making (A case study of closure)*. St. Louis, MO: Self-published.

Anderson, K. (2001–2010). Windows of opportunity: Bulding a multicultural community through art. Workshop.

Anderson, K. (2000a). *Expressive therapies: Studies in active imagination*. Paper, St. Louis Institute of Art Psychotherapy, St. Louis.

Anderson, K. (2000b). Wholistic practice: A systemic approach to mind, body, psyche and spirit in clinical social work. *Social Work 2000: Strategies to Succeed in the New Market Economy, NASW's Meeting of the Profession* (p. 10). Baltimore: NASW.

Anderson, K. (1996). Gangs, cults, and mind control [Presentation and accompanying material]. *Counseling Children and Adolescents*. St. Louis, MO.

Anderson, K., & Davis, B. M. (2008). Professional development model of cultural equity and racial literacy. St. Louis, MO.

Anti-Defamation League. (2005, Fall). Equal treatment, equal access: Raising awareness about people with disabilities and their struggle for equal rights. *ADL Curriculum Connections*. Anti-Defamation League.

Anti-Defamation League. (2000). *Religion in the public schools: Guidelines for a growing and changing phenomenon*. New York: Anti-Defamation League.

Axline, V. (1969). *Play therapy*. New York: Ballantine Books.

Bailey, S. (2001). *Beyond the "Gender Wars": A Conversation About Girls, Boys and Education*. Washington, DC: AAUW. Education Foundation.

Bauer, S. R., Sapp, M., & Johnson, D. (2000, December/January). Group counseling strategies for rural at-risk high school students. *The High School Journal*, 41–50.

Bauman, S., & Sachs-Kapp, P. (1998). School takes a stand: Promotion of sexual orientation workshops by counselors. *Professional School Counseling, 1*(3), 42–45.

BBC. (2009a). *Atheism at a glance*. Retrieved July 3, 2009, from http://www.bbc.co.uk/religion/religions/atheism/ataglance/glance_print.html

BBC. (2009b). *Paganism at a glance*. Retrieved July 3, 2009, from http://www.bbc.co.uk/religion/religions/paganism/ataglance/glance_print.html

Begnaud, A. E. (1964). Acadian exile. *Louisana History: The Journal of the Louisiana Historical Association, 5*(1), 5.

Bemak, F., Chung, R. C.-Y., & Siroskey-Sabdo, L. A. (2006). Empowerment groups for academic success: An innovative appoach to prevent high school failure for at-risk, urban African American girls. In S. M. Ravitch (Ed.), *School Counseling Principles: Multiculturalism and Diversity* (pp. 598–624). Alexandria, VA: American School Counselor Association.

Bennett, M. J. (1993). Towards ethnorelativism: A developmental model of intercultural sensitivity. In R. M. Paige (Ed.), *Education for the Intercultural Experience* (pp. 21–71). Yarmouth, ME: Intercultural Press.

Betensky, M. (1973). *Self-discovery through self-expression: The use of art in psychotherapy with children and adolescents*. Springfield, IL: Charles C Thomas Bickenback.

Bickenbach, J. E. (1993). *Physical disability and social policy*. Toronto, Ontario, Canada: University of Toronto.

Blatner, H. A. (1973). *Acting in: Practical application of psychodramatic methods*. New York: Springer Publishing Company.

Bonny, H. L. (1997). The state of the art of music therapy. *The Arts in Psychotherapy, 24*(1), 65–73.

Bryan, J., & Henry, L. (2008). Strengths-based partnerships: A school-family-community partnership approach to empowering students. *Professional School Counseling, 12*(2), 149–157.

Bryan, J., & Holcomb-McCoy, C. (2004). School counselors' perceptions of their involvement in school-family-community partnerships. *Professional School Counseling, 7*(3), 162–172.

Bryant, R. M., & Constantine, M. G. (2006). Multiple role balance, job satisfaction, and life satisfaction in women school counselors. *Professional School Counseling, 9*(4), 265–271

Buckel, D. (1998). *Stopping anit-gay abuse in public schools.* New York: Lambda Legal Defense and Education Fund.

Burnham, J. J., & Hooper, L. M. (2008). The influence of the war in Iraq on American youth's fears: Implications for professional school counselors. *Professional School Counseling, 11*(6).

Bye, L., Shepard, M., Partridge, J., & Alvarez, M. (2009). School social work outcomes: Perspectives of social workers and school administrators. *Children & Schools, 31*(2), 97–108.

Byrd, A. D., & Tharp, L. L. (2002). *Hair story: Untangling the roots of black hair in America.* New York: Macmillian Publishing Company.

Campbell, P. (2001). *Beyond the "Gender Wars": A Conversation About Girls, Boys and Education.* Washington, DC: AAUW. Education Foundation.

Carroll, L., & Anderson, R. (2002). Body piercing, tattooing, self-esteem, and body investment in adolescent girls. *Adolescence, 37*, 627–637.

Center for Applied Technology. (2010). *Fast facts for faculty.* Wakefield, MA: CAST.

Centers for Disease Control and Prevention. (2010). *Sexual and reproductive health of young people.* Retrieved January 18, 2010, from http://www.cdc.gov/Features/Sexual HealthData/

Centers for Disease Control and Prevention. (n.d.). *About teen pregnancy: adolescent reproductive health.* Retrieved January 18, 2010, from http://www.cdc.gov/reproductivehealth/adolescentreproductivehealth/AboutTP.htm

Cerf, C. (Ed.). (1987). *Free to be a family: A book about all kinds of belonging.* New York: Bantam.

Chapman, A. (2010). *Gender bias in education.* Retrieved March 8, 2010, from http://www.edchange.org/multicultural/papers/genderbias.html

Choate, L. (2009). Counseling adolescent girls for body image resilience: Strategies for school counselors. *Professional School Counseling, 10*(3), 317–326.

Christian Coalition. (2009, July). *Christian coalition: About us.* Retrieved June 18, 2009, from http://www.cc.org

Christian Educators Association International. (2009a). Declaration for public education. *Declaration for Public Education.* Westlake, OH: CEAI.

Christian Educators Association International. (2009b, July). *Who we are.* Retrieved June 18, 2009, from http://www.ceai.org

Clark, M., & Amatea, E. (2004). Teacher perceptions and expectations of school counselor contributions: Implications for program planning and training. *Professional School Counselor, 8*(2), 132–140.

Cooley, L. (2009). *The power of groups.* Thousand Oaks, CA: Corwin.

Coskun, M., & Zoroglu, S. S. (2009). Dissociative disorder following hospitalization and invasive medical procedures: A pediatric case report. *Archives of Neuropsychiatry, 46*, 30–33.

Cross, J. E., & Peisner, W. (2009). RECOGNIZE: A social norms campaign to reduce rumor spreading in a junior high school [Report]. *Professional School Counseling, 12*(5), 365–378.

Dallett, J. (1982). Active imagination in practice. In M. Stein (Ed.), *Jungian Analysis* (pp. 173–191). Lasalle: Open Court.

Davis, B. M. (2009). *The biracial and multiracial student experience: A journey to racial literacy.* Thousand Oaks, CA: Corwin.

Davis, B. M. (2006). *How to teach students who don't look like you: Culturally relevant teaching strategies.* Thousand Oaks, CA: Corwin.

Day-Vines, N. L. (2007). Wellness in the midst of adversity and tragedy. *Journal of Humanistic Counseling, Education and Development, 46,* 242–247.

Day-Vines, N. L., & Holcomb-McCoy, C. (2007). Wellness among African American counselors. *Journal of Humanistic Counseling, Education and Development, 46,* 82–97.

Denny, D. (2009). *Transgendered youth at risk for exploitation, HIV, hate crimes.* Retrieved July 5, 2009, from http://www.aidsinfonyc.org/q-zone/youth.html

DePaul, J., Walsh, M., & Dam, U. (2009). The role of school counselors in addressing sexual orientation in schools. *Professional School Counseling, 12*(4), 300–308.

Developmental Disabilities Assistance and Bill of Rights Act of 2000, Pub. L. No. 106-402, 114 Stat. 1677 (2000).

Diaz De Chumaceiro, C. L. (1996). Dual serendipity: Creative writing and self-analysis of associations to poetry and music. *The Arts in Psychotherapy, 77–81.*

Dickens, C. (1993). *A tale of two cities.* New York: Knopf Publishers. (Original work published 1859)

Disability History Museum. (n.d.). *Disability History Museum library.* Retrieved January 12, 2010, from http://www.disabilitymuseum.org/lib/

Doak, M. (1997, Spring). *Religious movements: Native American religion.* Retrieved July 11, 2009, from http://web.archive.org/web/200683009/religiousmovements.lib.virginia.edu

Dotson-Blake, K. R., Foster, V. A., & Gressard, C. F. (2009). Ending the silence of the Mexican immigrant voice in public education: Creating culturally inclusive family-school-community partnerships. *Professional School Counseling, 12*(3), 230–240.

Eaude, T. (2003). Shining lights in unexpected corners: New angles on young children's spiritual development. *International Journal of Children's Spirituality, 8*(2), 151–162.

Eliade, M. (2004). *Shamanism: Archaic techniques of ecstasy* (W. R. Trask, Trans.). Princeton, NJ: Princeton University Press.

Epstein, J., Sanders, M., Simon, B., Salinas, K., Jansorn, N., & Van Voorhis, F. (2002). *School, family, and community partnerships: Your handbook for action* (2nd ed.). Thousand Oaks, CA: Corwin.

Fein, A. H., Carlisle, C. S., & Isaacson, N. S. (2008). School shootings and counselor leadership: Four lessons from the field. *Professional School Counseling, 11*(4), 246–252.

First Amendment Center. (2009, July 14). *First Amendment Center: About.* (B. J. Buchanan, Ed.). Retrieved July 14, 2009, from http://www.firstamendmentcenter.org/about.aspx

First Amendment Center. (2003). *Teaching about religion in public schools: Where do we go from here?* Nashville, TN: The First Amendment Center.

Fisher, E. S., Komosa-Hawkins, K., Saldana, E., Thomas, G. M., Hsiao, C., Rauld, M., et al. (2008). Promoting school success for lesbian, gay, bisexual, transgendered, and questioning students: Primary, secondary, and tertiary prevention and intervention strategies. *The California School Psychologist, 13,* 79–91.

Flood, C. P., & Shaffer, S. (2000, November). Safe boys, safe schools. *WEEA Digest,* pp. 3–6.

Fusick, L., & Bordeau, W. C. (2006). Counseling at-risk Afro-American youth: An examination of contemporary issues and effective school-based strategies. In S. M. Ravitch (Ed.), *School counseling principles: Multiculturalism and diversity* (pp. 360–386). Alexandria, VA: American School Counselor Association.

Gaffney, D. A. (2006). The aftermath of disaster: Children in crisis. *Journal of Clinical Psychology: In Session, 62*(8), 1001–1016.

Gardner, H. (1983). *Frames of mind: The theory of multiple intelligences* (10th ed.). New York: Basic Books.

George, C. (2008). Solution-focused therapy: Strength-based counseling for children with social phobia. *Journal of Humanistic Counseling, Education and Development, 47*(Fall), 144–156.

Gerstein, L. H., Heppner, P. P., Ægisdottir, S., Leung, S.-M. A., & Norsworthy, K. L. (2009). *International handbook of cross-cultural counseling: Cultural assumptions and practicies worldwide.* Thousand Oaks, CA: Sage.

Gilligan, C. (1993). *In a different voice: Psychological theory and women's development.* Cambridge, MA: Harvard University Press.

GLSEN. (2009). *ThinkB4YouSpeak: Educator's guide.* New York: GLSEN.

Granados, C. (2000, December). Hispanic vs. Latino: A new poll finds that the term "Hispanic" is preferred. *Hispanic Magazine.*

Graves, K. (2004, August). *Resilience and adaptation among Alaskan native men.* Northampton, MA: Smith College School of Social Work.

Griffin, N. C. (1998). Cultivating self-efficacy in adolescent mothers: A collaborative approach. *Professional School Counseling, 1*(4), 53–58.

Halprin, S. (1996). *"Look at my ugly face": Myths and musings on beauty and other perilous obsessions with women's appearance.* New York: Penguin Books.

Harner, M. (1990). *The way of the Shaman.* San Francisco: HarperSanFrancisco.

Haynes, C. C. (2004, May 9). Accomodating Muslims in public schools: Where to draw the line? *Inside the First Amendment.* Retrieved April 26, 2010, from http://www.firstamendmentcenter.org/comentary.aspx?id=

Haynes, C. C., & Thomas, O. (2007). *Finding common ground: A First Amendment guide to religion in public schools.* Nashville, TN: The First Amendment Center.

Hede, M. (2009, June 18). *Hispanic vs. Latino.* Retrieved June 18, 2009, from http://www.hispanic-culture-online.com/hispanic-vs-latino.html

Heller, D. (1986). *The children's God.* Chicago, IL: University of Chicago Press.

Hendel, A. (2006). Restoring self-esteem in adolescent males. *Reclaiming Children and Youth, 15*(3), 175–178.

Henderson, K. (2009). *Overview of ADA, IDEA, and Section 504.* Retrieved January 18, 2010, from http://www.kidsource.com/kiscource/content3/ada.idea.html

Hindu American Foundation. (2010, January/February/March). Exploring the Hindu American identity. *Hinduism Today.*

Hindu American Foundation. (2009). *Hindu basics.* Retrieved July 10, 2009, from http://www.hafsite.org/resources/hinduism_101/hinduism_basics

History.com. (2009, July 5). *Major Christian denominations.* Retrieved July 5, 2009, from http://www.history.com/encyclopedia.do?articleId=227134

Hodge, D. R. (2004). Working with Hindu clients in a spiritually sensitive manner. *Social Work, 49*(1), 27–38.

Holcomb-McCoy, C. (2007). *School counseling to close the achievement gap: A social justice framework for success.* Thousand Oaks, CA: Corwin.

Holladay, J., English, T., Jackson, C., Kilman, C., & Thomason, R. (2009). *The ABCs of religion in schools.* Retrieved July 3, 2009, from http://www.tolerance.org/teach/printar.jsp?p=758&pi=apg

Hopfe, L. M. (1979). *Religions of the world.* Encino, CA: Glencoe Publishing.

Howard, K. A., Olberg, V., & Scott, H. (2006). School-based social justice: The achieving success identity pathways program. *Professional School Counseling, 9*(4), 278–287.

Huda. (2004, February 28). *About.Com: Islam.* Retrieved July 10, 2009, from http://islam.about.com/cs/divisions/f/shia_sunni.htm

Individuals with Disabilities Act of 2004, Pub. L. No. 108-446, 118 Stat. 2647 (2004).

Jackson, S., Pretti-Frontczak, K., Harjusola-Webb, S., Grisham-Brown, J., & Romani, J. M. (2009). Response to invervention: Implication for early childhood professionals. *Language, Speech and Hearing Services in Schools, 40,* 424–434.

Jarvis, C. (2008). Becoming a woman through wicca: Witches and wiccans in contemporary teen fiction. *Children's Literature in Education, 39,* 43–52.

Johnson, D. R. (1998). On the therapeutic action of creative arts therapies: The psychodynamic model. *The Arts in Psychotherapy,* pp. 85–98.

Kayer, H., & Sherman, J. (2009). At-risk ninth-grade students: A Psychoeducational group approach to increase study skills and grade point averages. *Professional School Counseling, 12*(2), 434–439.

Kim, B. S., Green, J. L. G., & Klein, E. F. (2006). Using story books to promote multicultural sensitivity in elementary school children. *Journal of Multicultural Counseling and Development, 34,* 223–234.

Kimmel, M. (2000, November). What about the boys. *WEEA Equity Resource Center Digest,* pp. 1–8.

Kindlon, D., & Thompson, M. (1999). *Raising Cain: Protecting the emotional life of boys.* New York: Ballantine.

Kluth, P. (2006). *Disability studies for teachers.* Retrieved January 18, 2010, from Center on Human Policy. Available from http://www.disabilitystudiesforteachers.org/files/DEAF_CULTURE.pdf

Korzenny, F., & Korzenny, B. A. (2005). *Hispanic marketing: A cultural perspective.* Burlington, MA: Elsevier/Butterworth-Heinemann.

LAMBDA. (2010). *When a student tells you they're gay.* Retrieved July 9, 2010, from http://www.lambda.org/student_comes_out.htm

LAMBDA. (2009). *Creating safer schools.* Retrieved July 5, 2009, from http://www.lambda.org/tips_safer_school.htm

Le Beau, B. F. (2005). *The atheist.* New York: New York University Press.

LeBlanc, S. (2010, Feburary 28). *The Cajuns—Arrival of the acadians.* Retrieved February 28, 2010, from http://www.thecajuns.com/acadians.htm

Leigh, I. W., & Brice, P. J. (2003). The visible and the invisible. In I. Leigh, P. Brice, J. D. Robinson, & L. C. James (Eds.), *Diversity in human interactions: The tapestry of America* (p. 182). New York: Oxford University Press.

Leuwerke, W. C., Walker, J., & Qi, S. (2009). Informing principals: The impact of different types of information on principal's perceptions of professional school counselors. *Professional School Counseling, 12*(4).

Lewis, O. (2007). *Seeking Native American spirituality and traditional religion: Read this first!* Retrieved July 11, 2009, from http://www.native-languages.org/religion.htm

Lewis, R., & Hatch, T. (2008). Cultivating strengths-based professional identities. *Professional School Counseling, 12*(2), 115–118.

Linton, J. (2005). Mental health counselors and substance abuse treatment: Advantages, difficulties, and practical issues to solution-focused interventions. *Journal of Mental Health Counseling, 27*(4).

Linton, S. (1998). *Claiming disability: Knowledge and identity.* New York: New York University Press.

Lippmann, W. (1997). *Public opinion* (2nd ed.). New Brunswick, CT: Transaction Publishers.

Logue, J. N. (2008). Violent death in american schools in the 21st century: Reflections following the 2006 Amish school shootings. *Journal of School Health, 78*(1), 58–61.

Lonborg, S. D., & Bowen, N. (2004). Counselors, communities, and spirituality: Ethical and multicultural considerations. *Professional School Counseling, 7*(5), 318–323.

MacDonald, D. (2004). Collaborating with students' spirituality. *Professional School Counseling, 7*(5), 293–300.

Maddow, R. (2010, January 13). *The Rachel Maddow show* [Television series]. New York: MSNBC.

Malchiodi, C. ((Ed.). (1999). *Medical art therapy with children.* London: Jessica Kingsley Publishers.

Malchiodi, C. (1998). *Understanding children's drawings.* London: Jessica Kingsley Publishers.

Malgady, R. G., & Zayas, L. H. (2001). Cultural and linguistic considerations in psychodiagnosis with Hispanics: The need for an empirically informed process model. *Social Work: Journal of the National Association of Social Workers, 46*(1), 39–49.

Markowitz, S. L. (1973). *What you should know about Jewish religion, history, ethics and culture.* Secaucus, NJ: Citadel Press.

Martin, J. (2003, April 11). *Teacher training issues for American Indian students.* Flagstaff, AZ: Southwest Indian Polytechnic Institute.

Martines, D. (2008). *Multicultural school psychology competencies: A practical guide.* Thousand Oaks, CA: Sage.

Mayo, J. B. (2008, October/November). Gay teachers' negotiated interactions with their students and (straight) colleagues. *The High School Journal,* pp. 1–10.

McAuliffe, G. (Ed.). (2008). *Culturally alert counseling: A comprehensive introduction.* Thousand Oaks, CA: Sage.

McClanahan, K. K., McLaughlin, R. J., Loos, V. E., Holcomb, J. D., Gibbins, A. D., & Smith, Q. W. (1998.) Training school counselors in substance abuse risk education techniques for use with children and adolescents. *Journal of Drug Education, 28*(1), 39–51.

McNiff, S. (2009). Cross-cultural psychotherapy and art. *Art Therapy, 26*(3), 100–106.

Merriam-Webster's collegiate dictionary (3rd ed.). (1973). Springfield, MA: Merriam-Webster.

Miller, K. M. (2006). The impact of parental incarceration on children: An emerging need for effective intervention. *Chid and Adolscent Social Work Journal, 23*(4), 472–486.

Milsom, A. (2006). Creativing Positive school experiences for students with disabilities. *Professional School Counselilng, 10*(1), 66–72.

Mireau, R., & Inch, R. (2009). Brief solution-focused counseling: A practical effective strategy for dealing with wait lists in commuity-based mental health services. *Social Work, 14*(1), 63–70.

Mitchell, N. A., & Bryan, J. A. (2007). School-family-community partnerships: Strategies for school counselors working with Caribbean immigrant families. *Professional School Counseling, 10*(4), 399–402.

Mogel, W. (2001). *The blessing of a skinned knee: Using Jewish teachings to raise self-reliant children.* New York: Penguin Compass.

Moleski, S. M., & Kiselica, M. S. (2005). Dual relationships: A continuum ranging from the destructive to the therapuetic. *Journal of Counseling and Development, 83*(1), 3+.

Molidor, C. E. (1996, May). Female gang members: A profile of agression and victimization. *Social Work,* pp. 251–257.

Moodley, R., & West, W. (Eds.). (2005). *Integrating traditional healing practices into counseling and psychotherapy.* Thousand Oaks, CA: Sage.

Nabors, L. A., & Lehmkuhl, H. D. (2004). Children with chronic medical conditions: Recommendations for school mental health clinicians. *Journal of Developmental and Physical Disabilities, 16*(1), 1–15.

National Campaign to Prevent Teen and Unplanned Pregnancy. (2010). *Get organized: A guide to preventing teen pregancy.* Retrieved January 18, 2010, from http://www.thenationalcampaign.org/resources/getorganized

National Center for Lesbian Rights. (2003). *Getting your school board on board: Pro talking points.* New York: National Center for Lesbian Rights.

National Coalition for the Homeless. (2008). *Education of homeless children and youth.* Washington, DC: National Coalition for the Homeless.

National Coalition for the Homeless. (2007). *Who is homeless.* Washington, DC: National Coalition for the Homeless.

National Universal Design for Leaning Task Force. (2010). *The facts for educators.* Retrieved January 18, 2010, from http://www.udl4allstudents.com

Nelson, J. A., & Bustamante, R. A. (2009, February 11). Preparing professional school counselors as collaborators in culturally competent school administration. *Connexions Module: m19617,* 8. National Council of Professors of Educational Administration.

Newman, L., & Sousa, D. (2000). *Heather has two mommies* (20th anniversary ed.). New York: Alyson Books.

Nord, W. (2007). *Ten suggestions for teaching about religions.* Chapel Hill: University of North Carolina.

O'Brien, B. (2009). *Buddhism basics.* Retrieved July 10, 2009, from http://buddhism.about.com/od/basicbuddhistteachings/u/basics.htm?p=1

Office of Disability Employment Policy. (2009). *Disability history: An important part of america's heritage.* Washington, DC: U.S. Department of Labor.

Office of Special Education and Rehabilitative Services. (2004). Individuals with Disabilities Act (IDEA). Washington, DC: U.S. Department of Education.

Olitzky, K. M., Rosman, S. M., & Kasakove, D. P. (1993). *When your Jewish child asks why: Answers for tough questions.* Hoboken, NJ: KTAV Publishing House.

Omizo, M. M., Omizo, S. A., & Honda, M. R. (1997). A phenomenological study with youth gang members: Results and implications for school counselors. *Professional School Counseling, 1*(1), 39–42.

Ontario Consultants on Religious Tolerance. (2009a). *Agnositicism.* Retrieved July 10, 2009, from http://www.religioustolerance.org/agnostic.htm

Ontario Consultants on Relgious Tolerance. (2009b). *An introduction to wicca.* Retrieved July 10, 2009, from http://www.religioustolerance.org/wic_intr.htm

Parents, Families, & Friends of Lesbians and Gays. (2009). *About our transgendered children.* Retrieved July 5, 2009, from http:// www.community.pflag.org

Pearlman, L. A., & Saatvitne, K. W. (1995). *Trauma and the therapist: Countertransference and vicarious traumatization in psychotherapy with incest survivors.* New York: W. W. Norton Company.

Pedrotti, J. T., Edwards, L. M., & Lopez, S. J. (2008). Promoting hope: Suggestions for school counselors. *Professional School Counseling, 12*(2).

Peterson, J. S. (2006). Addressing counseling needs of gifted students. *Professional School Counseling, 10*(1).

Phillips, L. (2001). *Beyond the "gender wars": A conversation about girls, boys, and education.* Washington, DC: AAUW Education Foundation.

Pipher, M. (1995). *Reviving Ophelia: Saving the selves of adolescent girls.* New York: Penguin Books.

Pollack, W. (2001). *Beyond the "gender wars": A conversation about girls, boys, and education.* Washington, DC: AAUW Education Foundation.

Ponterotto, J. G., Mendelowitz, D. E., & Collabolletta, E. A. (2008). Promotoing multicultural personality development: A strengths-based positive psychology worldview for schools. *Professional School Counseling, 12*(2).

Ponterotto, J. G., Utsey, S. O., & Pedersen, P. B. (2006). *Preventing prejudice: A guide for counselors, educators and parents* (2nd ed.). Thousand Oaks, CA: Sage.

Portman, T. A. A. (2009). Faces of the future: School counselors as cultural mediators. *Journal of Counseling and Development, 87*(1), 21–28.

Ravitch, S. M. (Ed.). (2006). *Multiculturalism and diversity: School counselors as mediators of culture.* Alexandria, VA: American School Counselor Association.

Reamer, F. G. (2003). Boundary issues in social work: Managing dual relationships. *Social Work, 48*(1), 121.

Religious Tolerance. (2009). Buddhism's core beliefs. Retrieved July 10, 2009, from http://www.religioustolerance.org/buddhism1.htm

Riva, M. T., & Haub, A. (2004). Group counseling in the schools. In J. DeLucia-Waack, D. Gerrity, C. Kalodner, & M. T. Riva (Eds.), *Handbook of group counseling and psychotherapy* (pp. 309–321). Thousand Oaks, CA: Sage.

Roaten, G., & Schmidt, E. (2009). Using experiential activities with adolescents to promote respect for diversity. *Professional School Counseling, 12*(4), 309–314.

Robertson, T., & Gunderson, D. (2003, August 20). *Rekindling the spirit: The rebirth of American Indian spirituality.* Bemidji: Minnesota Public Radio. Available from http://news.minnesota.publicradio.org/features/2003/03/18_gundersond_spiritualityone/

Romano, P. (2009, June 20). *Commemorating the past: An introduction to the study of historical memory.* Retrieved June 20, 2009, from http://greensborotrc.org/intro.doc

Rosenbaum, J. E. (2009). Patient teenagers? A comparison of the sexual behavior of virginity pledgers and matched nonpledgers. *Pediatrics, 123*(1), 110–120.

Saleebey, D. (1994). Culture, theory, and narrative: The intersection of meanings in practice. *Social Work, 39,* 351–359.

Salyers, K. M., & Ritchie, M. H. (2006). Multicultural counseling: An Appalachian perspective. *Journal of Multicultural Counseling and Development, 34*, 130–142.

Schevitz, T. (2002, November 26). FBI sees leap in anti-Muslim hate crimes. *San Francisco Chronicle*, p. 1.

Schutz, A. (1998). Assertive, Offensive, protective, and defensive styles of self-presentation: A taxonomy. *The Journal of Psychology, 132*(6), 611–629.

Sheldon, S. B. (2007). Improving student attendance with school, family, and community partnerships. *The Journal of Educational Research, 100*(5), 267–276.

Sherrod, M. D., Getch, Y. Q., & Ziomek-Daigle, J. (2009, August). The impact of positive behavior support to decrease discipline referrals with elementary students. *Professional School Counseling*, pp. 421–427.

Shiltz, T. (2005). *Males and eating disorders: Research.* Seattle, WA: National Eating Disorders Association.

Simcox, A. G., Nuijens, K. L., & Lee, C. C. (2006). School counselors and school psychologists: Collaborative partners in promoting culturally competent schools. *Professional School Counseling, 9*(4), 272–277.

Simpkinson, A. A., & Simpkinson, C. H. (1998). *Soul work: A field guide for spiritual seekers.* Ney York: HarperPerennial.

Singleton, G. E., & Linton, C. (2006). *Courageous conversations about race: A field guide for creating equity in schools.* Thousand Oaks, CA: Corwin.

Sink, C. (2010). *Current trends.* Retrieved January 16, 2010, from http://sites .google.com/site/chrissinkwebsite/history-of-school-counseling#TOC -Current-Trends

Sink, C. (2004). Spirituality and comprehensive school counseling programs. *Professional School Counselor, 7*(5), 309–315.

Sink, C., & Edwards, C. (2008). Supportive learning communities and the transformative role of professional school counselors. *Professional School Counselor, 12*(2), 108–114.

Sink, C. A., & Richmond, L. J. (2004). Introducing spirituality to professional school counseling. *Professional School Counseling, 7*(5), 291–292.

Sleeter, C. (2008). Critical family history, identity, and historical memory. *Educational Studies, 43*, 114–124.

Smart, J. F., & Smart, D. W. (2006, Winter). Models of disability: Implications for the counseling profession. *Journal of Counseling and Development, 84*, 29–40.

Smedley, A., & Smedley, B. D. (2005). Race as biology is fiction, race as social problem is real: Anthropological and historical perspectives on the social construct of race. *American Psychologist, 60*(1), 16–26.

Smith, J., & Niemi, N. (2007). Exploring teacher perceptions of small boys in kindergarten. *The Journal of Educational Research, 100*(6), 331–335.

Staver, M. D. (2005). Teachers' rights on public school campuses. In M. D. Staver, *Eternal vigilance: Knowing and protecting your religious freedom* (p. 17). Nashville, TN: Broadman and Holman.

Steen, S., Bauman, S., & Smith, J. (2007). Professional school counselors and the practice of group work. *Professional School Counseling, 11*(2), 72–80.

Stein, R. (2010, February 2). Abstinence-only programs might work, study says. *The Washington Post*, p. 1.

Stein, R. E. K., Westbrook, L. E., & Bauman, L. J. (1997). The questionnaire for indentifying children with chronic conditions: A measure based on a noncategorical approach. *Pediatrics, 99*, 513–521.

Stilson, J. (Director). (2009). *Good hair* [Motion Picture]. USA: Chris Rock Entertainment.

Stone, J. H. (Ed.). (2005). *Culture and disability: Providing culturally competent services.* Thousand Oaks, CA: Sage.

Strawser, S., Markos, P. A., Yamaguchi, B. J., & Higgis, K. (2000). A new challenge for school counselors: Children who are homeless. *Professional School Counseling, 3*(3), 162–172.

Stroh, H. R., & Sink, C. A. (2002). Applying APA's learner-centered principles to school-based group counseling. *Professional School Counseling, 6*(1), 71–78.

Sue, D. W., & Sue, D. (2008). *Counseling the culturally diverse: Theory and practice* (5th ed.). Hoboken, NJ: John Wiley & Sons, Inc.

Suris, J.-C., Jeannin, A., Chossis, I., & Michaud, P.-A. (2007). Piercing among adolescents: Body art as risk marker. *The Journal of Family Practice, 58*(2), 126–130.

Taliman, V. (1993). Article on the "Lakota Declaration of War." *News From Indian Country.*

Teaching Tolerance. (2001, September 13). *What is Islam?* Retrieved July 10, 2009, from http://www.tolerance.org/news/article_print.jsp?id=273

Thomas, V., & Ray. K. (2006). Counseling exceptional individuals and their families. *Professional School Counselor, 10*(1), 58–65.

Thorne, B. (2001). Part 4: What are the priorities: Setting an agenda for the future. In *Beyond the "gender wars": A conversation about girls, boys, and education* (pp. 32–45). Washington, DC: AAUW Education Foundation.

Turner, S., Reich, A., Trotter, M., & Siewart, J. (2009). Social skills efficacy and proactivity among Native American adolescents. *Professional School Counseling, 10*(2), 180–194.

U.S. Census Bureau. (2009, June 19). *Race and ethnic classifications used in census 2000 and beyond.* Retrieved June 19, 2009, from http://www.census.gov/population/www/socdemo/race/racefactcb.html

Uniformed Services University of the Health Sciences. (2008). *Helping children cope during deployment.* Bethesda, MD: Uniformed Services University of the Health Sciences.

Van Velsor, P. (2004). Revisiting basic counseling skills with children. *Journal of Counseling and Development, 82*, 313–318.

Velasquez, M. (2009). *Top ten reasons.* Retrieved June 20, 2009, from http://diversitydtg.com/articles/topten.html

Venegas, K. (2008, Summer). Using culturally based education to increase academic achievement and graduation rates. *NIEA News*, pp. 31–32.

Vonk, M. E. (2001). Cultural competence for transracial adoptive parents. *Social Work: Journal of the National Association of Social Workers, 46*(3), 246–255.

Watch Tower Bible and Tract Society. (1989). *Questions young people ask.* London: Watch Tower Bible and Tract Society.

Watch Tower Bible and Tract Society of Britain. (1995). *Jehovah's witnesses and education.* London: Watch Tower and Tract Society of Britain.

Weller, E. M. (2003). Making school safe for sexual minority students. *Principal Leadership Magazine*, p. 6.

Wilcoxon, S. A., Magnuson, S., & Norem, K. (2008). Institutional values of managed mental health care: Efficiency or oppression. *Journal of Multicultural Counseling and Development, 36*(3), 143–154.

Yalom, I. D. (1985). *The theory and practice of group psychotherapy* (3rd ed.). New York: Basic Books.

Yardley, M. (2008). Social work practice with pagans, witches, and wiccans: Guidelines for practice with children and youth. *Social Work, 53*(4), 329–336.

Zacharakis, J., Devin, M., & Miller, T. (2008). Political economy of rural school in the heartland. *Rural Special Education Quarterly,* pp. 16–22.

Index

CORWIN

A SAGE Company

The Corwin logo—a raven striding across an open book—represents the union of courage and learning. Corwin is committed to improving education for all learners by publishing books and other professional development resources for those serving the field of PreK–12 education. By providing practical, hands-on materials, Corwin continues to carry out the promise of its motto: **"Helping Educators Do Their Work Better."**